THE
ATOM BOMB

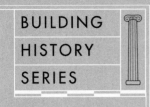
BUILDING
HISTORY
SERIES

THE
ATOM BOMB

by William W. Lace

Lucent Books, Inc., San Diego, California

Library of Congress Cataloging-in-Publication Data

Lace, William W.
    The atom bomb / by William W. Lace.
        p.   cm. — (Building history)
    Includes bibliographical references and index.
    Summary: Discusses the discovery of nuclear fission and the
development, testing, and use of the atomic bomb against Japan
during World War II.
    ISBN 1-56006-724-1 (hardback)
    1. Atomic bomb—History—Juvenile literature.   2. Nuclear
energy—History—Juvenile literature. [1. Atomic bomb—History.
2. Atoms. 3. Manhattan Project (U.S.)]
I. Title.   II. Building history series.
  QC773.A1 L27 2002
  355.8'25119—dc21
00-013094

Cover photos (clockwise from left): "Jumbo," the steel container
built to contain plutonium should the Trinity test fail; the detonation at Alamogordo; Ernest Lawrence monitors the operation of his
cyclotron.

CONTENTS

FOREWORD

Throughout history, as civilizations have evolved and prospered, each has produced unique buildings and architectural styles. Combining the need for both utility and artistic expression, a society's buildings, particularly its large-scale public structures, often reflect the individual character traits that distinguish it from other societies. In a very real sense, then, buildings express a society's values and unique characteristics in tangible form. As scholar Anita Abramovitz comments in her book *People and Spaces*, "Our ways of living and thinking—our habits, needs, fear of enemies, aspirations, materialistic concerns, and religious beliefs—have influenced the kinds of spaces that we build and that later surround and include us."

That specific types and styles of structures constitute an outward expression of the spirit of an individual people or era can be seen in the diverse ways that various societies have built palaces, fortresses, tombs, churches, government buildings, sports arenas, public works, and other such monuments. The ancient Greeks, for instance, were a supremely rational people who originated Western philosophy and science, including the atomic theory and the realization that the earth is a sphere. Their public buildings, epitomized by Athens's magnificent Parthenon temple, were equally rational, emphasizing order, harmony, reason, and above all, restraint.

By contrast, the Romans, who conquered and absorbed the Greek lands, were a highly practical people preoccupied with acquiring and wielding power over others. The Romans greatly admired and readily copied elements of Greek architecture, but modified and adapted them to their own needs. "Roman genius was called into action by the enormous practical needs of a world empire," wrote historian Edith Hamilton. "Rome met them magnificently. Buildings tremendous, indomitable, amphitheaters where eighty thousand could watch a spectacle, baths where three thousand could bathe at the same time."

In medieval Europe, God heavily influenced and motivated the people, and religion permeated all aspects of society, molding people's worldviews and guiding their everyday actions. That spiritual mindset is reflected in the most important medieval structure—the Gothic cathedral—which, in a sense, was a model of heavenly cities. As scholar Anne Fremantle so elegantly phrases it, the cathedrals were "harmonious elevations of stone and glass reaching up to heaven to seek and receive the light [of God]."

Our more secular modern age, in contrast, is driven by the realities of a global economy, advanced technology, and mass communications. Responding to the needs of international trade and the growth of cities housing millions of people, today's builders construct engineering marvels, among them towering skyscrapers of steel and glass, mammoth marine canals, and huge and elaborate rapid transit systems, all of which would have left their ancestors, even the Romans, awestruck.

In examining some of humanity's greatest edifices, Lucent Books' Building History series recognizes this close relationship between a society's historical character and its buildings. Each volume in the series begins with a historical sketch of the people who erected the edifice, exploring their major achievements as well as the beliefs, customs, and societal needs that dictated the variety, functions, and styles of their buildings. A detailed explanation of how the selected structure was conceived, designed, and built, to the extent that this information is known, makes up the majority of the volume.

Each volume in the Lucent Building History series also includes several special features that are useful tools for additional research. A chronology of important dates gives students an overview, at a glance, of the evolution and use of the structure described. Sidebars create a broader context by adding further details on some of the architects, engineers, and construction tools, materials, and methods that made each structure a reality, as well as the social, political, and/or religious leaders and movements that inspired its creation. Useful maps help the reader locate the nations, cities, streets, and individual structures mentioned in the text; and numerous diagrams and pictures illustrate tools and devices that bring to life various stages of construction. Finally, each volume contains two bibliographies, one for student research, the other listing works the author consulted in compiling the book.

Taken as a whole, these volumes, covering diverse ancient and modern structures, constitute not only a valuable research tool, but also a tribute to the human spirit, a fascinating exploration of the dreams, skills, ingenuity, and dogged determination of the great peoples who shaped history.

IMPORTANT DATES IN THE BUILDING OF THE ATOM BOMB

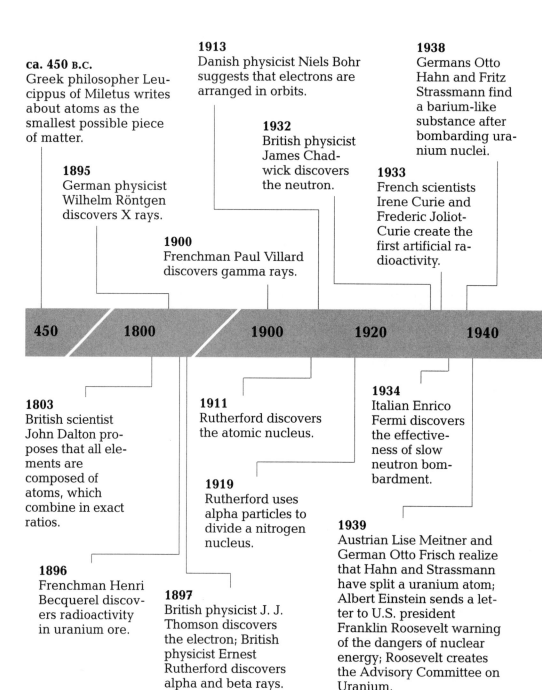

ca. 450 B.C.
Greek philosopher Leucippus of Miletus writes about atoms as the smallest possible piece of matter.

1895
German physicist Wilhelm Röntgen discovers X rays.

1900
Frenchman Paul Villard discovers gamma rays.

1913
Danish physicist Niels Bohr suggests that electrons are arranged in orbits.

1932
British physicist James Chadwick discovers the neutron.

1933
French scientists Irene Curie and Frederic Joliot-Curie create the first artificial radioactivity.

1938
Germans Otto Hahn and Fritz Strassmann find a barium-like substance after bombarding uranium nuclei.

450   1800   1900   1920   1940

1803
British scientist John Dalton proposes that all elements are composed of atoms, which combine in exact ratios.

1896
Frenchman Henri Becquerel discovers radioactivity in uranium ore.

1897
British physicist J. J. Thomson discovers the electron; British physicist Ernest Rutherford discovers alpha and beta rays.

1911
Rutherford discovers the atomic nucleus.

1919
Rutherford uses alpha particles to divide a nitrogen nucleus.

1934
Italian Enrico Fermi discovers the effectiveness of slow neutron bombardment.

1939
Austrian Lise Meitner and German Otto Frisch realize that Hahn and Strassmann have split a uranium atom; Albert Einstein sends a letter to U.S. president Franklin Roosevelt warning of the dangers of nuclear energy; Roosevelt creates the Advisory Committee on Uranium.

1941
British MAUD report convinces Roosevelt to establish the Top Policy Group to oversee atomic research; Japanese bomb the American naval base at Pearl Harbor, Hawaii (December 7).

1940
Frisch and Rudolf Peierls develop a gaseous diffusion method for separating U-235; American Ernest Lawrence develops an electromagnetic method to separate U-235; American Glenn Seaborg discovers the element plutonium.

1945
February: The "Dragon's Tail" experiment is performed at Los Alamos. April: The first supplies of U-235 are available for experiments at Los Alamos; Harry Truman learns about the atom bomb one day after Roosevelt's death (on April 12). July 16: The Fat Man plutonium bomb is tested at the Trinity site. July 24: General Groves drafts an order to use the atom bomb against Japan. July 26: The Potsdam Declaration calls on Japan to surrender. August 6: Little Boy is dropped on the Japanese city of Hiroshima. August 9: Fat Man is dropped on Nagasaki. August 14: The Japanese surrender ends World War II.

| 1940 | 1941 | 1942 | 1943 | 1944 | 1945 |

1942
June: The Army Corps of Engineers is given a role in atomic research; the project takes the name "Manhattan" from the Corps of Engineers' office in New York. August 20: Seaborg extracts the first sample of pure plutonium. September: General Leslie Groves is named chief military officer of the Manhattan Project; construction begins at the Oak Ridge, Tennessee, plant. October: J. Robert Oppenheimer is named as the director of manufacturing the atom bomb. November: Oppenheimer and Groves select Los Alamos, New Mexico, as the site for bomb research. December 2: Fermi creates the first self-sustaining chain reaction.

1943
March: The Los Alamos research site opens. April: Seth Neddermeyer proposes an implosion weapon; the uranium gun and plutonium bomb are nicknamed Thin Man and Fat Man. September: Testing of explosives begins at Los Alamos. December: The Thin Man uranium gun is redesigned, nicknamed "Little Boy."

1944
September: The first plutonium reactor begins operation at Hanford, Washington. November: Work begins at the Trinity test site.

INTRODUCTION

The predawn hours are cold, even in mid-July, in the Jornada del Muerto desert of south-central New Mexico. At about 5:15 on the morning of July 16, 1945, those scientists and technicians not tinkering with equipment or peering at dials stood here and there rubbing their hands together, from the cold or nervousness or both. In a few minutes, the world's first atom bomb test would occur.

The test of the plutonium device, nicknamed Fat Man, was the culmination of years of intense scientific and engineering work—and the expenditure of $2 billion. Some observers were fearful that, despite all the calculations, the bomb would not work. Others, realizing the tremendous power that would be unleashed—and the use to which that power would be put—were fearful that it would.

The location had been chosen with care, a desolate valley west of the Oscura Mountains. Its name—Journey of Death—was appropriate. The nearest village was thirty miles to the north. The dry, barren terrain was unbroken except for a few scrubby mesquite and yucca. The water—what there was of it—was bitter and alkaline.

The valley's natural inhabitants—scorpions, snakes, and a few hardy jackrabbits—had been forced of late to share their dwelling place with hundreds of scientists and soldiers living in tents and prefabricated huts. The normally still landscape had hummed with activity, the center of which on this July morning was a one-hundred-foot-high tower with a corrugated iron shed on top. In the shed sat "the gadget," as the bomb had come to be called. It was roughly spherical, about six feet in diameter, with five thousand pounds of high explosives packed around a thirteen-pound plutonium core. Wires sprouted from the surface, trailed down the tower, and snaked across the desert floor to various observation posts.

ANXIOUS MOMENTS

The command center was in S-10,000, a fortified shelter ten thousand yards (5.7 miles) south of ground zero. Here, the project's leaders waited nervously. Were they far enough away from ground zero? No one knew how powerful the explosion would be, if, indeed, there was any explosion at all. Days before, a test device without the plutonium core had yielded doubtful results.

J. Robert Oppenheimer, the director of the project, thought the blast would be equal to three hundred tons of the conventional explosive TNT. George Kistiakowski, who had overseen the basic design of the bomb, predicted fourteen hundred tons. Edward Teller, who would later develop the hydrogen bomb, chose an optimistic forty-five thousand tons. Enrico Fermi, who in 1942 had created the world's first man-made nuclear reaction, had suggested—jokingly, he said—that the blast would ignite the atmosphere and destroy all of New Mexico, if not the entire world. "We were reaching into the unknown," wrote General Thomas Farrell, "and we did not know what might come of it."[1]

The countdown was conducted by physicist Sam Allison, whose words over the loudspeakers were inexplicably accompanied by classical music picked up from a radio station

Scientists and workmen prepare to raise the plutonium device, nicknamed Fat Man, to the top of a one-hundred-foot-high tower in the Jornada del Muerto desert.

in California. He periodically called out the time: minus three minutes, minus two minutes. "Lord, these things are hard on the heart,"[2] Oppenheimer said.

THE LAST MINUTE

At minus one minute, a signal rocket was fired. Twenty miles to the north, on Compañia Hill, Teller and other observers covered their eyes with dark welder's glasses. At minus forty-five seconds, the automatic timing device was activated. Now, only Donald Hornig, one of the team's youngest members, could stop the test by cutting a wire leading to the bomb.

Minus ten seconds, a gong sounded in the bunker and everyone inside took cover . . . nine . . . eight . . . seven. As the countdown ended, Allison suddenly feared that the energy from the blast might somehow be conducted to the microphone he held. At minus one second, he dropped the microphone and yelled, "Zero!"[3]

J. Robert Oppenheimer, the director of the atom bomb project, predicted that the explosion would be equal to three hundred tons of TNT.

The desert night immediately gave way to a brilliance never before seen by humans. "It blasted," wrote scientist Isidor Rabi. "It pounced; it bored its way right through you."[4]

Seconds later, the sound of the blast and the accompanying shock wave reached the shelters. Some observers who had not taken precautions were knocked to the ground. They scrambled up to look at the yellow-purple fireball mushrooming in the distance.

For a moment, all they could do was gaze, awestruck. Then, the tension broke. Some men cheered; others slapped one another on the back. Some broke out bottles of liquor in celebration. Still others remained quiet, sobered by the enormity of what they had accomplished and what it might mean, for both good and evil.

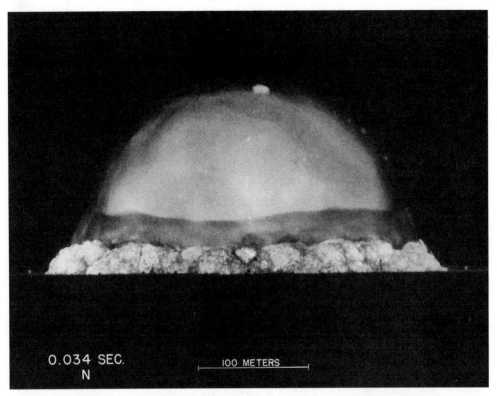

0.034 SEC.
N

|___100 METERS___|

The bomb is seen here less than a second after detonation. The explosion lit the predawn desert sky with a brilliance never before seen by humans.

Oppenheimer, a troubled genius who had driven his team and himself relentlessly, felt relief, but also a sense of foreboding. As he looked on what was in great measure his creation, into his mind came a line from the Bhagavad Gita, a sacred Hindu poem: "I am become death, the shatterer of worlds."[5]

DIVIDING THE INDIVISIBLE

When ancient Greek philosophers advanced the notion that everything in the universe—from the soil to the soul—is made up of incredibly tiny particles, they had no way to put their theories to a test. Only twenty-five centuries later did scientists, after painstaking research and experimentation, affirm this concept of matter, unlock the secrets within nature's building blocks, and use those secrets to fashion history's most destructive weapon.

EARLY THEORIES

Leucippus of Miletus, a philosopher writing in about 450 B.C., was the first person known to argue that if a piece of matter were divided, then divided again and again, theoretically a point would be reached at which it could no longer be divided. It would have been reduced to its basic components. Leucippus's pupil, Democritus of Abdera, named these tiny bits of matter *atomos*, meaning indivisible. Democritus wrote that not only tangible substances but also thought and emotion consisted of atoms, which moved constantly through a void and regrouped themselves randomly.

Greek philosopher Aristotle believed that all matter is made up of only four elements.

In the next century, however, Aristotle disagreed with the atomic theory. He rejected the idea of a purely mechanical universe, holding instead that creation is the result of a rational plan and that people, as rational beings, can come to know that plan through their senses. Accordingly, he wrote in his treatise, *Physics,* that all matter is made up of four elements—earth, air, fire, and water—that are evident to human senses.

Centuries later, Christian writers adapted Aristotle's concept to their theology, finding that it meshed nicely with their doctrine of a divine creator. Since Christian doctrine came to dominate European thinking, the atomic theory was thrust into obscurity for about fifteen hundred years.

NEWTON'S VIEW

Scientists began once more to suspect the existence of atoms in the late 1600s. Sir Isaac Newton's discovery of gravity revived the notion of a universe governed by strict mechanical laws. Newton himself believed that atoms existed, but he agreed with the ancient Greeks that they were the smallest possible bits of matter. He wrote in 1704,

> It seems probable to me that God in the Beginning form'd Matter in solid, massy, hard, impenetrable, moveable Particles, of such Sizes and Figures, and with such other Properties, and in such Proportion to Space, as most conduced to the End for which he form'd them; and that these primitive Particles being Solids, are incomparably harder than any porous Bodies compounded of them; even so very hard, as never to wear or break in pieces; no ordinary Power being able to divide what God himself made one in the first Creation.[6]

DALTON'S LAW

There was little evidence that atoms existed, however, until the work of British chemist John Dalton in the early 1800s. In the mid-1600s another British chemist, Robert Boyle, had defined the difference between basic elements (oxygen, lead, gold, sulfur, etc.) and compounds (materials formed by the mixture of two or more elements). Dalton noted that when two or more elements can combine to form more than one substance, the ratio of the weights of the elements can always be expressed in whole numbers. In other words, while carbon monoxide results from three pounds of carbon burned with

Sir Isaac Newton agreed with the Greek theory that atoms were the smallest bits of matter.

four pounds of oxygen, it takes exactly double the amount of oxygen to produce carbon dioxide. Thus, Dalton reasoned that the different substances resulted from combinations of the atoms of the elements used.

Dalton was never able to discover how, if matter is made up of atoms, the atoms are held together. The answer lay in something he never suspected: Atoms themselves are made up of still smaller particles.

The first indications that atoms are something other than minute, indivisible building blocks that somehow latch on to one another came later in the 1800s during electricity experiments in Great Britain. Chemist Humphry Davy found that passing electric current through some compounds would break the compounds into their respective elements. This suggested that the elements were held together by electrical force.

FARADAY'S EXPERIMENTS

Davy's successor, Michael Faraday, performed experiments passing electric current through various compounds. Faraday noted that the current caused a substance to be deposited on the electrode, the metal conductor leading from the source of electricity. He also observed that a fixed amount of current would cause a fixed deposit of material to form. For instance, no matter what kind of carbon solution he used or what type of electrode, the same electrical charge yielded the same amount of carbon. Faraday thus concluded that each molecule of a compound has exactly the same electrical charge and, furthermore, that atoms have some sort of electrical properties that enable them to combine with other atoms. Since scientists knew that electricity results from a combination of positive and negative charges, Faraday's conclusions suggested that atoms, rather than being the smallest possible bits of matter, might contain positive and negative particles.

THE DISCOVERY OF X RAYS

Suspicion was one thing; proof was another. Even a half-century after Faraday's experiments, Robert Cecil, the chancellor of Oxford University, said in 1894 that the questions about atoms "remain surrounded by a darkness as profound as ever."[7] A series of groundbreaking discoveries over the next few years would begin to shed light on the inner workings of the atom.

In 1895, German physicist Wilhelm Röntgen was working with a cathode ray tube, a glass tube from which all air had been removed and which would light up, or fluoresce, when an electrical current was passed through it. One day, he noticed that when the tube was switched on, a barium compound accidentally left

THE NEWTONIAN VIEW

The idea that atoms are not indivisible but are made up of separate particles was slow to gain acceptance in the scientific world despite growing evidence. Even James Clerk Maxwell, whose groundbreaking work in electricity and magnetism in the 1800s would be shown in the next century to depend on subatomic particles, defended Sir Isaac Newton's view that atoms were immutable bits of matter that behaved in a mechanical, predictable manner. This quotation from Maxwell is found in *The Making of the Atomic Bomb* by Richard Rhodes.

> Though in the course of ages catastrophes have occurred and may yet occur in the heavens, though ancient systems may be dissolved and new systems evolved out of their ruins, the [atoms] out of which [the sun and the planets] are built—the foundation stones of the material universe—remain unbroken and unworn. They continue to this day as they were created—perfect in number and measure and weight.

on an adjacent table glowed. Clearly, rays of some sort were passing through the tube and the air to the barium. Even more startling, he found that when he put his hand in the path of these rays, he could see the outline of his bones. Since rays like this were completely unknown, he called them X rays.

Frenchman Henri Becquerel, experimenting with X rays a year later, made another monumental discovery. Again, it was partially by accident. Seeking to find whether any substances that had been shown to fluoresce also emitted X rays, he wrapped photographic plates in black paper, then placed the fluorescing material on top of the paper and exposed the setup to direct sunlight. He thought that sunlight would activate the X rays, which would penetrate the paper and fog the photographic plate.

German physicist Wilhelm Röntgen discovered X rays when he noticed that he could see the outline of his bones when he put his hand next to a cathode ray tube.

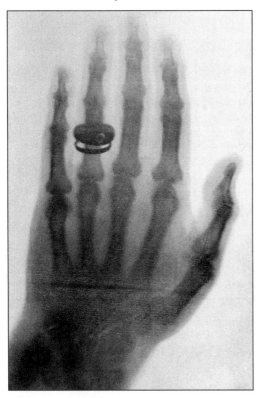

A SURPRISE RESULT

After several substances failed to produce X rays, Becquerel tried pitchblende, a uranium salt. When he developed the plate he saw the silhouette of the salt crystals sharply outlined. He tried to repeat the experiment a few days later, but the day was overcast. He placed the paper-wrapped plate, sprinkled with pitchblende, in a drawer. After two days he developed the plate, thinking that, because of the feeble light, the images on the plate would be dim. On the contrary, they were just as sharp as those exposed to bright sunlight. Clearly, the uranium was emitting rays even though it was not stimulated by light.

Meanwhile, in Great Britain, another important discovery was made. Physicists had argued for years over whether the rays generated in the cathode ray tube were light waves or particles of matter. In 1897, J. J. Thomson placed a tube between aluminum plates of opposite electrical charges. When the top plate was negative, the rays were bent down. When the top plate was positive, the rays were bent upward. Since it was known that two negative charges repel each other, Thomson concluded that the rays were negatively charged bits of matter.

Further experiments showed that these particles were a thousand times lighter than hydrogen, the smallest known atom. Thomson concluded, therefore, that they were parts of atoms, and he named them electrons. The ancient notion of atoms as homogeneous substances had finally been disproved.

More progress was made in 1898 when the French team of Marie and Pierre Curie, studying Becquerel's X rays, determined that substances in pitchblende other than uranium were responsible for the phenomenon. They managed to isolate two new elements—polonium and radium—and Marie Curie gave the emission of rays the name by which it is still known, radioactivity.

Back across the English Channel, physicist Ernest Rutherford began experimenting with radioactivity. He discovered that at least two types of rays were being released. He named the first type "alpha" rays. They were less penetrating and could be blocked with a thin piece of aluminum foil. The second type, "beta" rays, had a much higher power of penetration. In 1900 Frenchman Paul Villard discovered a third ray, which he named the "gamma" ray. It had far more penetrating power than even beta rays. Decades later, beta and gamma radiation would be one of the deadlier aspects of the atom bomb, "burning" human tissue it came into contact with.

ISOTOPES

Rutherford and an associate, chemist Frederick Snoddy, identified another phenomenon when studying the radioactive element thorium, which gave off a mysterious gas. As the thorium gave off radiation, it changed into a new and highly radioactive form of element that in turn disappeared, yielding nonradioactive argon gas.

They had discovered that the same element may have different atomic and chemical characteristics. Snoddy named the varieties of standard elements "isotopes," and isotopes were to play a crucial role in the development of the atom

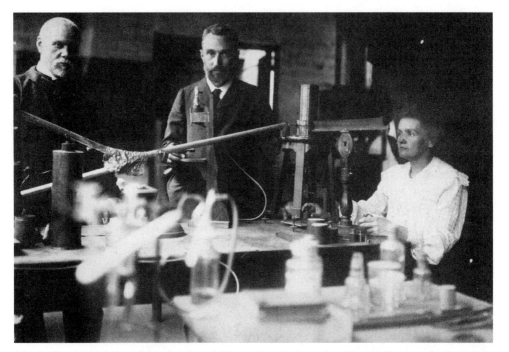

Marie Curie (right) and her husband Pierre (center) work with a colleague in their lab. The French chemists discovered polonium and radium, and Marie came up with the name radioactivity to identify the rays emitted by the two elements.

bomb. Furthermore, he calculated that the amount of energy released during radioactivity was much greater than that yielded by ordinary chemical reactions. In a 1903 paper, after presenting his calculations, he wrote, "The energy of radioactive change must therefore be at least twenty thousand times, and may be a million times, as great as the energy of any molecular change."[8]

Rutherford sensed that such force, if ever released, could be tremendously destructive. An associate at Cambridge University later recalled that Rutherford made a "playful suggestion that, could a proper detonator be found, it was just conceivable that a wave of atomic disintegration might be started through matter, which would indeed make this old world vanish in smoke."[9]

Snoddy had similar concerns, but was more serious in his approach. Although he saw the theoretical possibilities of atomic energy, he reasoned that, if it had not already occurred in nature, it probably would never be achieved by science. At a lecture in 1904, he said,

It is probable that all heavy matter possess—latent and bound up with the structure of the atom—a similar quantity of energy to that possessed by radium. If it could be tapped and controlled what an agent it could be in shaping the world's destiny! The man who puts his hand on the lever by which a parsimonious [stingy] nature regulates so jealously the output of this store of energy would possess a weapon by which he could destroy the earth if he chose. . . . [However,] the fact that we exist is a proof that [such a massive release of energy] did not occur; that it has not occurred is the best possible assurance that it never will. We may trust Nature to guard her secret.[10]

ATOMIC MODELS

Scientists had discovered that atoms consisted of particles but could only guess at how those particles were arranged. They knew that, since electrons had a negative charge, other portions of the atom must have a positive charge. Such opposite charges would be necessary to hold the atom together. Also, in order to account for the known mass of atoms, the positively charged particles would have to be very large in relation to the extremely small electrons.

Thomson suggested a model in which the tiny, negatively charged electrons were scattered within a larger, positively charged sphere. This came to be called the "plum pudding" model. A Japanese physicist, Hantaro Nagaoka, advanced a "Saturnian" model, suggesting that electrons revolved around a positively charged central core like moons around the planet Saturn.

English physicist Ernest Rutherford suggested that with the proper detonator, a wave of atomic disintegration might be started through matter.

Rutherford was able to clarify the picture somewhat. In 1906, at McGill University in Montreal, he had observed that when alpha rays were sent in a concentrated beam through a slit onto a photographic plate, they would yield a sharp image. When the slit was covered with an extremely thin sheet of mica, however, the image was fuzzy. The rays should have been able to penetrate the mica easily. Something was deflecting them.

Years later, back in England at Manchester University, Rutherford took up the problem again. He directed an associate, Hans Geiger (who later invented the Geiger counter to measure radioactivity), and student Ernest Marsden in an experiment. Alpha particles were beamed through a piece of gold foil. On the side of the foil opposite the source of radiation, the researchers positioned a glass plate coated with zinc oxide. When alpha particles struck the plate, they would create tiny flashes of light visible under a microscope.

DISCOVERING THE NUCLEUS

The scientists painstakingly charted the flashes. Most of the particles penetrated through the gold foil in a straight line. Some were deflected slightly, as might be expected when encountering a weak charge from a small part of an atom of the plum pudding model, but a few were deflected as much as forty-five degrees. Intrigued, Rutherford told Marsden to see whether any of the particles did not penetrate the foil but were reflected back. To Marsden's great surprise, some of the alpha particles were reflected back from the foil more than ninety degrees.

Rutherford was astounded. He said later,

> It was quite the most incredible event that has ever happened to me in my life. It was almost as incredible as if you fired a 15-inch shell at a piece of tissue paper and it came back and hit you. On consideration I realised that this scattering backwards must be the result of a single collision, and when I made calculations I saw that it was impossible to get anything on that order of magnitude unless you took a system in which the greatest part of the mass of the atom was concentrated in a minute nucleus.[11]

On March 7, 1911, Rutherford announced his discovery of the nature of the nucleus, which he said consisted of positively charged particles that he later called protons. More experiments showed that the distance from the electrons to the nucleus was enormous in comparison to the diameter of the nucleus. In other words, atoms consisted mostly of empty space.

Rutherford's model of the atom had some problems. If electrons whizzed around the nucleus like planets around the sun, what kept them there? According to the mechanical laws of physics, they should gradually lose their energy and spiral into the nucleus. It was left to Niels Bohr, a young Danish scientist, to answer the question of how the electrons are arranged.

Working on the theoretical frameworks provided earlier by Max Planck and Albert Einstein, Bohr suggested in 1913 that electrons exist in stable orbits, emitting their electrical charge not continuously but in short amounts known as quanta. According to quantum mechanics, electrons were gathered around the nucleus in a series of stable orbits, like a series of spheres nested within one another.

MOONSHINE

In the early 1930s, even with all the discoveries that had been made about subatomic particles and their energy, scientists were doubtful that the energy could ever be put to practical use. Even Ernest Rutherford, the man who discovered the nucleus and first divided the atom, was skeptical. On September 12, 1933, the London *Times* gave this summary of one of Rutherford's lectures, as quoted in *The Making of the Atomic Bomb* by Richard Rhodes.

> What, Lord Rutherford asked in conclusion, were the prospects 20 or 30 years ahead. . . . We might in these processes [bombardment with neutrons] obtain very much more energy than the proton supplied, but on the average we could not expect to obtain energy in this way. It was a very poor and inefficient way of producing energy, and anyone who looked for a source of power in the transformation of the atoms was talking moonshine [wishful thinking].

SPLITTING THE ATOM

Rutherford, meanwhile, continued to study the nucleus. During an experiment, his associate Marsden bombarded hydrogen with alpha particles in order to chart the scattering effect. He noticed, however, that even when the hydrogen was removed, tiny flashes of light on a screen indicated that some was still present.

Rutherford could not believe that hydrogen had been given off by the radioactive material itself. Only alpha and beta particles had thus far been discovered, and they had been identified as helium nuclei and electrons, respectively. Rutherford tried bombarding several gases with little result. Then he tried plain air and was surprised when several flashes appeared. Since air

Danish scientist Niels Bohr theorized that electrons were gathered around the nucleus in stable orbits and emitted their electrical charge in short amounts known as quanta.

is 78 percent nitrogen, he thought that nitrogen might be the cause. Sure enough, when he used pure nitrogen, the flashes multiplied. "From the results so far obtained," he wrote, "it is difficult to avoid the conclusion that the long-range atoms arising from collision of [alpha] particles with nitrogen are not nitrogen atoms but probably atoms of hydrogen. . . . If this be the case, we must conclude that the nitrogen atom is disintegrated."[12]

Rutherford had achieved what few had thought possible. He had split the atom. What had happened was that the alpha particle, a helium nucleus with four protons, had collided with a nitrogen nucleus of fourteen protons. The collision knocked out one proton—the hydrogen nucleus causing the flash—and what remained was an isotope of oxygen with seventeen protons. Rutherford tried similar experiments with other elements and got similar results. The heavier elements resisted the bombardment, however. The light, slow-moving alpha particle lacked the energy to penetrate the electrical field around the heavier nuclei.

The means to penetrate heavier elements was not discovered until 1932. Scientists had long been aware of the difference between atomic numbers and atomic weights. Atomic weights were based on the ratios in which elements combined, with the lightest element, hydrogen, given the atomic weight of one. Helium was four, carbon was twelve, and so on. Atomic numbers, on the other hand, were related to the amount of electric charge in the nucleus. Hydrogen, again, had a number of one, but helium was two and oxygen was eight. If there were only eight protons in the nucleus of oxygen, what made up the rest of the weight?

THE NEUTRON

Rutherford speculated in 1920 that the difference might be made up of neutral particles formed by the union of protons and electrons. He said that should such a neutral particle—the neutron—ever be discovered, it could be the tool needed to probe the atomic nucleus, since it would not be repelled by the electrical field surrounding it.

German scientists had observed that beryllium, when bombarded with alpha particles, gave off an intense radiation that they assumed to be gamma rays. Marie Curie's daughter, Irene, and her husband Frederic Joliot used this radiation to knock protons out of paraffin wax.

Rutherford and an associate, James Chadwick, did not believe that gamma rays could have such an effect. Gamma rays had been shown to deflect electrons, but protons were almost two thousand times heavier. Chadwick conducted his own experiments using the beryllium radiation not only on paraffin but on other materials. The effect was the same. Whatever was knocking the protons out of the material being bombarded had to be more penetrating than an alpha particle but larger in mass than gamma rays. "In order to explain this great penetrating power of the radiation," Chadwick wrote, "we must further assume that the particle has no net charge. . . . We may suppose it [to be] the 'neutron' discussed by Rutherford."[13]

Chadwick had discovered the third major component of matter. Now the difference between atomic weight and atomic number was obvious. A helium nucleus had a positive charge of two, but the addition of two neutrons to two protons gave it the observed atomic weight of four. Four neutrons along with three protons gave lithium its atomic weight of seven.

Chadwick had also given nuclear physics one of its most valuable tools. "A beam of thermal neutrons," wrote American physicist Philip Morrison, "moving at about the speed of sound [which would generate only about one-fortieth of a volt] . . . produces nuclear reactions in many materials much more easily than a beam of protons of millions of volts [of] energy, traveling thousands of times faster."[14] Another noted scientist, Hans Bethe, said that Chadwick's discovery of the neutron separated history from prehistory as far as nuclear physics was concerned.

Over the centuries, researchers had painstakingly confirmed the existence of

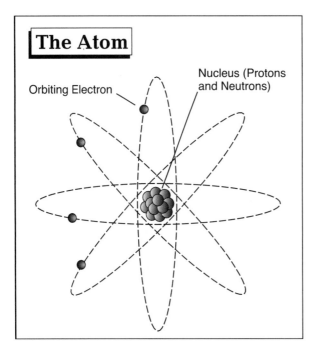

The Atom

Orbiting Electron

Nucleus (Protons and Neutrons)

SONG TO THE NEUTRON

James Chadwick's discovery of the neutron made him famous throughout the world of physics. Weeks after his findings were published, the scientists and students at Niels Bohr's Institute for Theoretical Physics in Copenhagen, Denmark, hailed Chadwick's achievement and included a song about it in a show celebrating the institute's tenth anniversary. George Gamow translated the song in his book *Thirty Years That Shook Physics.*

Now a reality,

Once but a vision

What classicality,

Grace and precision!

Hailed with cordiality,

Honored in song,

Eternal Neutrality

Pull us along!

the atom, discovered its basic structure, and furnished the tools with which to make further discoveries. Science now had the keys to unlock the tremendous energy stored within the atom. How long would it take, and what uses would that energy be put to? The chain of events that would force answers to those questions was already in progress. One year after Chadwick's discovery of the neutron, Adolf Hitler became chancellor of Germany. The threat of another world war loomed large, and with it came the specter that humanity would unleash the newfound atomic energy on itself.

ACCELERATION

By the early 1930s, scientists had discovered enough about the atom to think they might be able to liberate the energy locked within it. Whether they would be able to control that energy and to use it—for either peaceful or destructive purposes—was another matter. Much more experimentation was yet to be done, and the approaching war made such research increasingly urgent. Finally, with the outbreak of World War II, the race to build the world's first atom bomb became a matter of survival.

A ONE-SIDED RACE

Although no one knew it at the time, the race to build the bomb would be one-sided. This was in large part because of the anti-Jewish beliefs of Adolf Hitler and his Nazi Party. Hitler's racial policies would deprive Germany of many outstanding Jewish scientists or other scientists with Jewish ties. These men and women—Albert Einstein, Niels Bohr, Leo Szilard, Hans Bethe, Otto Frisch, Lise Meitner, Edward Teller, and Enrico Fermi among them—were to become the heart of wartime atomic research in the United States.

In 1933, however, war was only a cloud on the horizon in Paris where Irene Curie and Frederic Joliot-Curie were studying the effects of bombarding aluminum with alpha particles, causing it to release neutrons. To their surprise, the aluminum continued to give off particles after the alpha source was removed. The aluminum nucleus (thirteen protons, fourteen neutrons) had captured the alpha particle (two protons, two neutrons) and emitted one neutron. The result was an unstable and radioactive isotope of phosphorus. For the first time in history, radioactivity had been created artificially.

Researchers now began to believe in the possibility of harnessing the atom. In March 1934, Hungarian-born Leo Szilard took out the first of several patent applications anticipating nuclear energy. He foresaw the possibility that bombarding a nucleus with neutrons could induce a chain reaction, meaning the nucleus would release neutrons that would collide with other nuclei releasing still more neutrons at an increasing tempo with a corresponding release of energy. Szilard described how a sufficient amount of a substance, which he called the "critical mass," would be needed to sustain the reaction and how "if the thickness [of material containing the reaction] is larger than the critical value [of the reaction] . . . I can produce an explosion."[15]

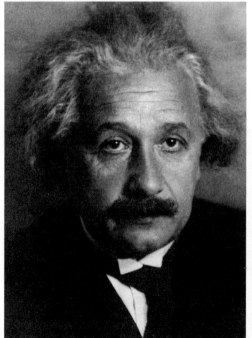

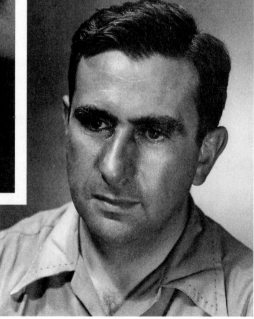

Hitler's racial policies deprived Germany of many outstanding Jewish scientists such as Albert Einstein (left) and Edward Teller (right), who would form the backbone of atomic research in the United States.

ENRICO FERMI

Szilard was dealing with theory. Meanwhile, in Rome, Enrico Fermi was irradiating, or bombarding with neutrons, different elements to try to make them radioactive. Heavy elements tended to gain a neutron, transforming themselves into isotopes of an even heavier element. Fermi thought that the heaviest known element, uranium at atomic number 92, would be transformed by neutron bombardment into a previously unknown element with an atomic number of 93.

The new substance was isolated from the uranium, then tested. It bore no resemblance to any of the elements just below uranium in atomic number, so Fermi assumed it was element 94. As it turned out, he had not run enough tests and had just missed making a profound breakthrough. He did, however,

A LAST THRILL

In 1933, when the husband and wife team of Irene Curie and Frederic Joliot-Curie became the first researchers to induce radioactivity artificially, one of the first persons they wanted to share their triumph with was Irene's mother. Marie Curie, who with husband Pierre had discovered radium and polonium years earlier, was terminally ill with leukemia from too much exposure to radiation over the years. Frederic Joliot, as quoted by Pierre Biquard in *Frederic Joliot-Curie,* described the scene.

> Marie Curie saw our research work and I will never forget the expression of intense joy which came over her when Irene and I showed her the first artificially radioactive element in a little glass tube. I can still see her taking in her fingers (which were already burnt with radium) this little tube containing the radioactive compound—as yet one in which the activity was very weak. To verify what we had told her she held it near a Geiger-Müller counter [a device to measure radioactivity] and she could hear the rate meter giving off a great many "clicks." This was doubtless the last great satisfaction of her life.

Marie Curie died on July 4, 1934.

make one important finding in the course of his experiments. Puzzled why more activity resulted when a substance was irradiated on a wooden rather than a marble table, he discovered that the hydrogen in the wooden table had slowed the neutrons and that slow neutrons were more effective.

Two years later, Niels Bohr explained this phenomenon. A fast neutron, he said, tends to go all the way through a target nucleus, causing no change. A slow neutron striking a nuclear particle, on the other hand, loses some of its energy, slows down, and is captured, creating the heavier isotope of the original substance. This unstable isotope then decays through radioactivity, but the result is a stable element still heavier than the original. Furthermore, Bohr said, the nuclei of heavier elements are not rigid; rather, because of the opposing forces of the binding energy and the protons' tendency to repel one another, they are more like drops of liquid, which can change shape.

But was uranium under irradiation really producing a new element heavier than uranium? In November 1938, two German physicists, Otto Hahn and Fritz Strassmann, attempted to find out. Irradiating uranium produced substances that they sought to separate from the uranium chemically. They found that by far the greatest separation was achieved with barium. Since barium was known to separate radium from uranium ores, they thought they had produced isotopes of radium, element 88. There was just one problem, as Hahn wrote to his Austrian colleague Lise Meitner: The radium isotopes had characteristics similar to barium. "We understand it [uranium] can't really break up into barium. . . . So try to think of some other possibility."[16]

MEITNER'S INSIGHT

Meitner immediately knew what had happened. The uranium nucleus had split. This was the discovery that Fermi had missed years before. Hahn and Strassmann's substance was acting like barium because it *was* barium. Meitner and her nephew, fellow scientist Otto Frisch, figured out how the nucleus had split while walking near a resort in Sweden. Using Bohr's liquid-drop model of the atom as a starting point, they theorized that the wobbly uranium nucleus, absorbing a slow neutron, became even more unstable. As its wobbling increased, it elongated into two sections connected by a thin waist, looking something like a dumbbell. Eventually, the waist would break and the nucleus would split.

SUDDEN INSIGHT

The history of science is full of discoveries that have been made by researchers who had a sudden insight. Such a hunch served Enrico Fermi well when he discovered the ability of slow neutrons to induce fission. His description of this discovery is quoted by fellow physicist and biographer Emilio Segrè in *Enrico Fermi: Physicist.*

Enrico Fermi.

I will tell you how I came to make the discovery which I suppose is the most important one I have made. We were working very hard on the neutron-induced radioactivity and the results we were obtaining made no sense. One day, as I came into the laboratory, it occurred to me that I could examine the effect of placing a piece of lead before the incident neutrons. Instead of my usual custom, I took great pains to have the piece of lead precisely machined. I was clearly dissatisfied with something: I tried every excuse to postpone putting the piece of lead in its place. When finally, with some reluctance, I was going to put it in place, I said to myself: "No, I do not want this piece of lead here; what I want is a piece of paraffin [a waxy substance used as a sealant or for waterproofing]." It was just like that with no advance warning, no conscious prior reasoning. I immediately took some odd piece of paraffin and placed it where the piece of lead was to have been.

The experiment showed that the hydrogen in the paraffin slowed the neutrons and that slow neutrons greatly increased fission.

Meitner and Frisch concluded that since Hahn and Strassmann, starting with uranium (ninety-two protons), had wound up with barium (fifty-six protons), the other part of the nucleus must have been formed into krypton (with the remaining thirty-six protons). The total number of neutrons in these two substances, however, was at least six short of those in uranium. Those six neutrons, then, had to have been released in the form of an enormous amount of energy.

Back in his laboratory in Copenhagen, Frisch put the theory to the test. The experiment worked. Among those he showed the results to was an American biologist, William A. Arnold, who gave the process the name by which it has been known ever since—nuclear fission. Arnold later wrote,

> Later that day Frisch looked me up and said, "You work in a microbiology lab. What do you call the process in which one bacterium divides into two?" And I answered, "binary fission." He wanted to know if you could call it "fission" alone, and I said you could.[17]

When a uranium atom splits, it breaks up into atoms whose mass is less than that of the original uranium. The remaining mass is converted into enormous energy.

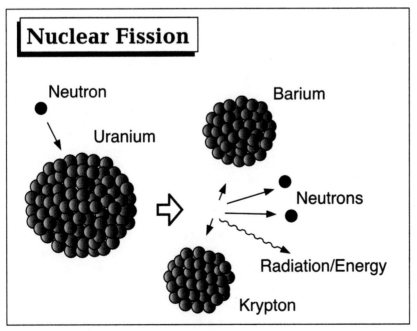

Nuclear Fission

Neutron

Barium

Uranium

Neutrons

Radiation/Energy

Krypton

The question still remained why slow neutrons increased fission in uranium but not in similar elements. Again, Bohr was able to supply the answer. In its natural state, most uranium had nuclei with 92 protons and 146 neutrons. Added together, they gave uranium its atomic weight of 238; in scientific shorthand, it was known as U-238. However, there were small amounts of two isotopes present, called U-234 and U-235 because they had four and three fewer neutrons, respectively. Bohr showed that it was the isotopes in uranium that responded to the slow neutrons.

Bohr's discovery had great meaning for the eventual development of an atomic weapon. The huge amount of natural uranium that would have been necessary to generate a large explosion would have made a bomb impractical. U-235, however, makes up less than 1 percent of uranium, so a much smaller amount would be needed. The trick, of course, was how to separate the two in sufficient quantities.

The possibilities presented by the discovery of fission, coupled with the timing, worried many in the scientific community. Frisch's experiments took place in January 1939, when Hitler had already taken over Austria and Czechoslovakia and was threatening Poland. Details of fission, wrote Szilard to a friend, "ought to be kept secret from the Germans." [18]

SENSING DANGER

In March, Szilard, Fermi, and others met in the office of George Pegram, a dean at New York's Columbia University. They decided that, with atomic weapons now a possibility, however remote, they should inform the U.S. government. On March 17, Fermi met in Washington with a small group of military officers and civilian scientists. They were unimpressed.

By July the situation in Europe had worsened and war was expected at any time. Szilard explained the situation to Alexander Sachs, who occasionally served as an economic adviser to President Franklin D. Roosevelt. Szilard was stunned when Sachs said that the matter should be taken directly to the White House. Furthermore, Sachs agreed to personally take to Roosevelt a letter from Albert Einstein warning the president of the possibility of Nazi scientists developing a nuclear weapon.

Sachs received the letter in mid-August, but the long-anticipated European war finally broke out on September 1, and it was October 11 before Sachs could see Roosevelt. Sachs did not read Einstein's lengthy letter aloud, but instead gave Roosevelt his own summary. He ended by quoting physicist Francis Aston, who had said in 1936,

> Personally I think there is no doubt that sub-atomic energy is available all around us, and that one day man will release and control its almost infinite power. We cannot prevent him from doing so and can only hope that he will not use it exclusively in blowing up his next door neighbor.

A PERSUASIVE ARGUMENT

When it became more evident in the late 1930s that atomic weapons might be possible, some scientists urged that subsequent discoveries be kept secret. They worried that Germany might use the knowledge to build a bomb for Nazi leader Adolf Hitler. Leo Szilard and Isidor Rabi had such fears and tried to enlist Enrico Fermi to their way of thinking, but Fermi took a lot of convincing. Rabi went to talk to Fermi and later reported Fermi's less-than-enthusiastic response to Szilard, who was quoted in *Leo Szilard: His Version of the Facts,* edited by Spencer R. Weart and Gertrude Weiss Szilard.

> I asked him [Rabi]: "Did you talk to Fermi?" Rabi said, "Yes, I did." I said, "What did Fermi say?" Rabi said, "Fermi said 'Nuts!'" So I said, "Why did he say 'Nuts?'" And Rabi said, "Well, I don't know, but he is in and we can ask him." So we went over to Fermi's office, and Rabi said to Fermi, "Look, Fermi, I told you what Szilard thought and you said 'Nuts' and Szilard wants to know why you said 'Nuts'?" So Fermi said, "Well . . . there is the remote possibility that neutrons may be emitted in the fission of uranium and then of course possibly a chain reaction can be made." Rabi said, "What do you mean by 'remote possibility'?" and Fermi said, "Well, ten per cent." Rabi said, "Ten per cent is not a remote possibility if it means that we may die of it. If I have pneumonia and the doctor tells me that there is a remote possibility that I might die, and it's ten per cent, I get excited about it."

To Sachs, Roosevelt replied "Alex, what you are after is to see that the Nazis don't blow us up."[19] The president called an aide, and before the day was out an Advisory Committee on Uranium had been appointed. It marked the U.S. government's first official involvement in atomic research.

The committee first met on October 21. Among the scientists was Edward Teller, a Hungarian immigrant who taught at George Washington University and kept in close touch with Fermi at Columbia. When the subject of money came up, Teller asked for $6,000 for graphite for the Columbia experiments. He later wrote, "My friends blamed me because the great enterprise of nuclear energy was to start with such a pittance. They haven't forgiven me yet."[20]

THE κ FACTOR

Fermi had been at work for most of the year on experiments he hoped would lead to a reaction in which neutrons released by the splitting of uranium nuclei would, in striking other nuclei, split them in turn, resulting in the release of other neutrons that would split still other nuclei, and so on. His goal was a "self-sustaining" nuclear reaction, one in which the rate of neutron release was constant or increasing. This in turn would generate a constant or increasing level of energy. Fermi designated this neutron reproduction factor as k. The k factor yielded by his experiments had to be at least 1.0—one released neutron causing the release of one additional neutron—to achieve a sustained reaction.

Fermi's experiments consisted of arranging layers of uranium and graphite, a form of the element carbon that was used to moderate, or slow down, the neutrons. Fermi dubbed his arrangement, which could encompass several cubic yards of material, a "pile," and the term soon took its place in the growing jargon of nuclear science. The principle of the experiment was that when the pile was large enough, it would reach critical mass and undergo fission spontaneously. The reaction could be kept from going "supercritical" and exploding by sliding control rods made of a neutron-absorbing substance into the pile.

While Fermi worked steadily throughout 1940, other researchers were just as active. Frisch, now working at the University of Birmingham in England, teamed with fellow German refugee Rudolf Peierls. Peierls had worked out a formula for calculating the amount of U-238 needed to form a critical mass. Now,

German soldiers advance into Poland as war breaks out in Europe on September 1, 1939. Soon President Roosevelt received warning of the possibility that the Nazis would develop a nuclear weapon.

he and Frisch applied it to U-235. To Frisch's amazement, he wrote, the answer "was very much smaller than I had expected; it was not a matter of tons, but something like a pound or two."[21]

Intrigued, the pair worked out what energy might be generated by the explosion of such a mass and found that it would yield temperatures equal to the inside of the sun. They wondered, then, if such an amount of U-235 could be separated from U-238. To find out, Frisch experimented with a method in which diffusion of uranium gas in a tube could separate the isotopes. He and Peierls calculated that about a hundred thousand such tubes, if perfected, could render a pound of U-235 in a matter of weeks. "At that point," wrote Frisch, "we stared at each other and realized that an atomic bomb might be possible after all. . . . The cost of such a plant would be insignificant compared with the cost of the war."[22]

MAGNETIC SEPARATION

Meanwhile, Ernest Lawrence of the University of California at Berkeley was considering another method of separating uranium isotopes. Years before, he had invented the cyclotron, a machine consisting of powerful magnets arranged in a circle in such a way as to accelerate an alpha particle. Lawrence

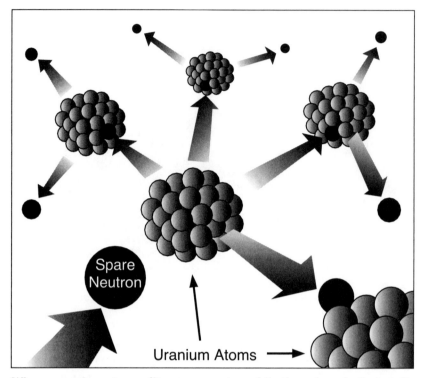

Spare
Neutron

Uranium Atoms ⟶

When a uranium atom splits, spare neutrons hit other atoms in their path, which in turn release more neutrons, creating a chain reaction.

reasoned that if the magnetic field were used in the same way on a stream of uranium ions, the lighter U-235 ions would separate and could be captured.

Berkeley was also home base for Edwin McMillan and Philip Abelson. Investigating a substance left behind by the slow neutron bombardment of uranium, they discovered that, instead of an isotope of uranium as previously thought, it was an isotope of a new element heavier than uranium. They named it neptunium for the planet in the next orbit from Uranus, for which uranium had been named.

Glenn Seaborg, a Berkeley chemist, took the process a step further. Theoretically, the unstable neptunium should decay into a still heavier element. In March 1940, Seaborg was able to isolate this element 94 and found that it undergoes fission even more efficiently than U-235. Seaborg named his discovery after the planet next in line after Neptune and thus, ironically, after the Greek god of the dead: plutonium.

By mid-1941, the U.S. government had taken a greater role in nuclear research. In June 1940, President Roosevelt had established the National Defense Research Council, headed by Vannevar Bush of the Carnegie Institute. The new organization, reporting directly to the president, absorbed the old Uranium Committee and, a year later, became the Office of Scientific Research and Development (OSRD), with almost total authority over government science and engineering projects.

Even so, the outlook for an atomic weapon was dim in the fall of 1941. Fermi and Szilard tested a nuclear pile at Columbia, but it yielded a disappointing k factor of .87. A review of atomic research for the National Academy of Science headed by Arthur Compton of the University of Chicago was doubtful that a weapon could be developed in time to affect the war. Later, Compton wrote, "The government's responsible representatives were . . . very close to dropping fission studies from the war program."[23]

The momentum to continue came from Great Britain. A report, code-named MAUD, on British research was delivered to

In 1940 President Roosevelt established the National Defense Research Council. Later, the Council became the Office of Scientific Research and Development and gained almost total authority over government science and engineering projects.

the United States in October. The British stated flatly that they thought it was possible to make an effective uranium bomb with about twenty-five pounds of active material and that such a bomb would be equivalent to eighteen hundred tons of TNT. Research should be centered in the United States, the report said, because of the resources available there.

Roosevelt reacted to the report by naming what he called the Top Policy Group to govern all decisions relating to atomic research. The group consisted of only five men: the vice president; the secretary of war; the army chief of staff; Bush; and the president of Harvard University, chemist James Conant. Roosevelt assured Bush that he would find the necessary funds to continue research.

In November, the National Academy of Science delivered another report, this one more optimistic yet still expressing reservations. The likelihood of an atom bomb, it said, was "as sure as any untried prediction based upon theory and experimentation can be."[24] Nevertheless, the academy recommended that research on the methods of manufacturing U-235 be accelerated. Bush delivered the report to Roosevelt on November 27, 1941. Ten days later, Japanese planes bombed the U.S. naval base at Pearl Harbor and the United States was at war.

The shock of Pearl Harbor shook off any lingering hesitation. In January 1942, the various research programs were placed under direct control of Section One of the OSRD, headed by Compton. One of Compton's early decisions was to move all U-235 and plutonium research to the same location. No one at Berkeley, Princeton, or Columbia wanted to move, so Compton cut through the squabbling and chose his own university, Chicago.

In May, reacting to another favorable research report and the increasing danger that Germany might beat the Allies to an atomic weapon, Roosevelt committed the United States to an all-out effort. "I think the whole thing should be pushed not only in regard to development, but also with due regard to time," the president wrote. "This is very much of the essence."[25]

BRINGING IN THE ARMY

Conant had estimated that the effort to produce an atom bomb might cost as much as $500 million and involve engineering and construction projects on an unprecedented scale. Bush decided in June to involve the U.S. Army directly, and the Corps

U.S. sailors fight fires aboard two burning battleships during the bombing of Pearl Harbor. The attack shook off any lingering hesitation about producing the atom bomb.

of Engineers—the branch of the army concerned with construction—opened an office in New York, giving it the innocuous name of the Manhattan Engineer District Office. This office eventually would give the entire enterprise the name by which it would be known to history—the Manhattan Project.

The all-out push quickly brought results. Seaborg had moved to Chicago in June to continue his work on plutonium, the extraction of which was made difficult because an amount as small as an ounce would be dispersed throughout tons of uranium ore. Seaborg subjected fifteen milliliters of uranium nitrate hexahydrate to a series of meticulous chemical procedures designed to extract pure plutonium. Tiny crystals thought to contain the plutonium were precipitated chemically, dissolved in acid, and evaporated to a point where only about one milliliter— about three-hundredths of a fluid ounce—was left. The sample grew ever smaller under a series of reactions until, on August 20, only plutonium remained, a tiny pinkish speck barely visible without a microscope.

An enormous amount of work lay ahead before the speck could translate into the pounds needed for a critical mass, but the first and most important step had been made. Distillation of pure plutonium was possible. Throughout the rest of the day, everyone associated with the lab—even the burly workers who had hauled heavy equipment and lead bricks—got a chance to peek through the microscope at what they had helped bring into existence.

On a vastly larger scale, Fermi was still seeking to show that a chain reaction could be achieved, sustained, and controlled. He, too, had moved to Chicago and had set up laboratories under the grandstand of Stagg Field, the football stadium at the University of Chicago, which had dropped the sport some years earlier. He and his team built a series of test piles, refining both materials and methods, getting ever closer to achieving a k factor of 1.0 or higher. After a k of .995 was reached, Fermi decided that the time had come to build a full-sized pile. Construction began on a special building outside the city that would house the experiment, but a dispute with construction labor unions caused delays. Fermi finally convinced Compton to allow the pile to be built in a doubles squash court under the Stagg Field grandstand.

BUILDING THE PILE

Crews worked almost around the clock under the direction of Walter Zinn and Herbert Anderson, both of whom had moved from Columbia with Fermi. Experiments had shown that the most efficient shape for the pile was a sphere that would consist of seventy-six layers of graphite bricks. Between each layer of plain graphite, or "dead" bricks, were two layers of graphite into which holes had been bored and filled with compressed uranium oxide; the graphite acted as a moderator to slow down the neutrons emitted by the uranium. At various points in the pile, control rods were placed that, when extracted, would allow fission to occur.

Thanks to the acquisition of higher quality graphite and uranium, however, Fermi was able to omit twenty layers of bricks. (The finished product, instead of being spherical, would be egg shaped, twenty feet high, and twenty-five feet wide.) The work was physically demanding. The blocks of graphite, the same material that pencil lead is made of, were heavy, slippery, and dirty. Graphite dust coated everything and everyone. Furthermore, with the onset of winter, the unheated labs grew frigid.

Finally, on the morning of December 2, the pile was ready for the crucial test. With about thirty people looking on, wrapped in coats and scarves against the bitter cold, Fermi ordered the control rods withdrawn inch by inch. As the rods were pulled out, neutron activity increased.

Fermi worked slowly and carefully, measuring neutron intensity at each step and inserting the rods periodically to let the pile "cool." At last, shortly before 4:00 P.M. he ordered the main safety rod, called ZIP, withdrawn. "This is going to do it,"[26] he told Compton.

GOING CRITICAL

As fission activity increased, the clicks of the Geiger counters measuring radiation grew more rapid, finally merging into a

The pile that would demonstrate the ability to control a nuclear chain reaction takes shape in a squash court under the Stagg Field grandstand. When completed, it was twenty feet high and twenty-five feet wide.

steady roar. A technician switched over to a device that registered the intensity of the reaction on a chart, much like an electrocardiogram registers heartbeats. Later, Anderson recalled the scene:

> When the switch was made, everyone watched in the sudden silence the mounting deflection of the recorder's pen. It was an awesome silence. Everyone realized the significance of that last switch; we were in the high intensity regime and the counters were unable to cope with the situation anymore. Again and again, the scale of the recorder had to be changed to accommodate the neutron intensity which was increasing more and more rapidly. Suddenly Fermi raised his hand. "The pile has gone critical," he announced. No one present had any doubt of it.[27]

The pile was allowed to run for four and a half minutes and had generated only one half-watt of power. Everyone there knew, however, what a momentous step had been taken. Humans had generated and controlled the release of atomic energy. Physicist Eugene Wigner described the feeling:

> For some time we had known that we were about to unlock a giant; still, we could not escape the eerie feeling

The main safety rod, called ZIP, is withdrawn from the graphite pile. The pile then went critical, and the momentous step of generating and controlling atomic energy was achieved.

HITLER AND THE BOMB

In May 1942, just as the United States decided to mount an all-out effort to develop an atom bomb, Nazi Germany made the opposite decision. German scientists were doubtful a bomb could be made before the end of the war, and resources were needed elsewhere. In addition, Nazi leader Adolf Hitler did not have the faith in scientific research that his American counterpart, Franklin D. Roosevelt, did. In his book *Inside the Third Reich*, Albert Speer, Hitler's chief weapons expert, writes,

> Hitler had sometimes spoken to me about the possibility of an atom bomb, but the idea quite obviously strained his intellectual capacity. He was also unable to grasp the revolutionary nature of nuclear physics. . . . Hitler was plainly not delighted with the possibility that the earth under his rule might be transformed into a glowing star. Occasionally, however, he joked that the scientists in their unworldly urge to lay bare all the secrets under heaven might some day set the globe on fire. But undoubtedly a good deal of time would pass before that came about, Hitler said; he would certainly not live to see it.

Accordingly, Germany dropped their atomic research program. Hitler turned out to be correct. He committed suicide in May 1945, four months before two atom bombs were dropped on Japan.

when we knew we had actually done it. We felt as, I presume, everyone feels who has done something that he knows will have very far-reaching consequences which he cannot foresee.[28]

It had taken five centuries from when atoms were first envisioned to discover the last of its three main building blocks, the neutron. Now, only ten years later, the energies contained in the atom had been found, set loose, and controlled. It was, however, just a beginning. Fashioning these beginnings—a speck of plutonium and a half-watt of power generated by a uranium pile—into a weapon would require an even greater effort, and a world at war waited for the results.

3

THE GADGET

When Enrico Fermi produced and maintained a chain reaction in December 1942, he confirmed what most scientists already believed: An atom bomb was possible. The question now was not if the bomb could be built, but how. The problems to be solved by the Manhattan Project were not theoretical but practical and straightforward. First, how could enough fissionable material—uranium 235 or plutonium—to form a critical mass be manufactured? Second, what devices—able to be dropped from an airplane—could be built that would bring lumps of those materials together in such a way as to produce an explosion?

THE PRODUCTION PROBLEM

The U.S. government had not waited until the success of Fermi's experiment before launching an all-out effort. The most immediate problem was the production of U-235 and plutonium. There were hardly enough minute specks on hand for experimentation, let alone the as-yet-undetermined number of pounds necessary for a weapon. Several methods for producing fissionable materials were possible, but no one knew which one would prove best. This uncertainty, coupled with the fear that Nazi Germany would build a bomb first, led Vannevar Bush and his Military Policy Committee that had been established in June 1943 to pursue all the possibilities at once.

Scientists had identified four potential methods of separating U-235 from the heavier U-238. The first was a high-speed centrifuge, a machine that spun rows of tubes of the gas uranium hexafluoride, or hex, in a circle so rapidly that gravity forced the heavier form of uranium to the bottom. The second was liquid thermal diffusion. Developed by physicist Philip Abelson, the process involved passing liquid hex between sources of heat on one side and cold on the other. The lighter U-235 tended to rise toward the top, where it could be scooped off.

The third method was gaseous diffusion, the method by which the first separation of U-235 and U-238 had been achieved. Hex gas was filtered through a series of ultrathin filters containing microscopic holes, and the lighter molecules of U-235 passed through more rapidly than the heavier U-238. At each stage, the part of the gas passing through a membrane was pumped to the next stage and filtered once more while the part remaining was removed.

USING THE CYCLOTRON

The fourth method, and the most promising in 1942, was the electromagnetic separation using Ernest Lawrence's cyclotron. It worked on the principle that an atom moving through a magnetic

The fear that Germany would build an atom bomb first led Vannevar Bush and his Military Policy Committee to pursue all methods of producing fissionable materials at once.

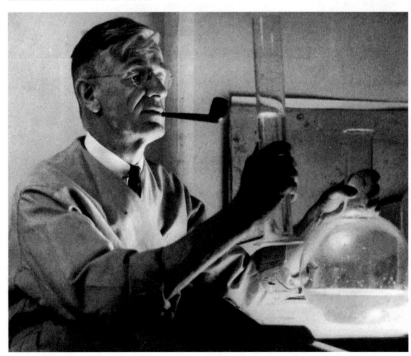

field moves in a circle according to its mass; the lighter the atom, the tighter the circle. Lawrence had shown that if a gaseous uranium compound were put through a strong magnetic field, the U-235 and U-238 ions, after traveling in a four-foot semicircle, would separate by about three-tenths of an inch and a collector could be placed to catch the U-235.

The production of plutonium relied on a radioactive pile such as the one Fermi built in Chicago. While some U-238 nuclei fissioned when absorbing a neutron, others did not, resulting in an isotope of neptunium that then decayed into plutonium. The self-sustaining chain reaction, therefore, was not only a source of energy but also a method of producing plutonium that took far less time than the long, complex chemical route taken by Seaborg.

Lawrence adjusts his cyclotron, which would be used in the most promising method of separating U-235 from U-238.

Production of enough of either substance would require manufacturing on a massive scale. Lawrence, running his thirty-seven-inch cyclotron at Berkeley, had produced one hundred micrograms of U-235. Hundreds of millions times more would be needed for a bomb. Thousands of workers and hundreds of millions of dollars would be required. The project called for a strong administrator, someone who could push through red tape and get things done. Leslie Groves was the ideal choice. Groves, the army's deputy chief of construction, had a reputation as a tough leader who drove those under him as well as himself mercilessly in order to get a job done.

A TOUGH LEADER

Like most officers during the war, Groves wanted an overseas combat assignment. He was angry about his new role, but that was before he knew exactly what it was. He complained to his superior, General Brendon Somervell. Later, Groves wrote,

> "If you do the job right," General Somervell said carefully, "it will win the war."

> Men like to recall, in later years, what they said at some important or possibly historic moment in their lives. . . . I remember only too well what I said to General Somervell that day.

> I said, "Oh."[29]

Groves was promoted to general and soon had the Manhattan Project in high gear. He bought tons of uranium ore that had been sitting in storage since being shipped to the United States from Africa by Belgium to protect it from seizure by Germany. He wrangled a top-priority rating for the project, threatening to go to Roosevelt if he didn't get it.

OAK RIDGE

Groves also pushed through the purchase of fifty-two thousand acres of land on the Clinch River in Tennessee. Within a few months, this quiet wilderness area would become a human anthill of activity. Construction crews threw up a town—named Oak Ridge—and then began work on the enormous buildings in which U-235 was to be produced. Large electromagnetic devices (named calutrons for the University of California, where

General Leslie Groves (left) confers with J. Robert Oppenheimer (right). As the army's deputy chief of construction, Groves was the ideal choice to oversee the Manhattan Project.

they were developed) were arranged in huge ovals nicknamed "racetracks." They were housed in a complex called Y-12 that eventually would contain more than 250 buildings. The two main buildings together covered more space than twenty-two football fields.

The plant housing the gaseous diffusions equipment was even larger. It required thousands of tanks up to one thousand gallons in capacity. The main building was four stories tall and covered forty-two acres, more than twice the size of the main electromagnetic buildings.

HANFORD

Groves decided that U-235 production and plutonium production should be kept separate. He did not want to run the risk of a nuclear explosion during the plutonium process that would wipe out the U-235 effort as well. He chose a 780-square-mile site in eastern Washington state along the Columbia River, whose plentiful supply of cold water would be used to cool the uranium piles. A power line and the Union Pacific Railroad crossed the site, thereby solving power and transportation problems.

Construction at the site, called the Hanford Engineering Works after a nearby village, was on a scale just as massive as in Tennessee. Three separation plants were built, each eight hundred feet long, sixty-five feet wide, and eighty feet tall. Because the buildings were so long and narrow, construction workers named them "Queen Marys" after the British ocean liner, although the real *Queen Mary* was only about a fifth that length.

DIFFICULT CONDITIONS

Life at both Hanford and Oak Ridge was difficult. Hanford was on a sandy plain, and the constant construction kicked up clouds of gritty dust that got into hair, eyes, clothing, and even food. The chief problem at Oak Ridge was mud resulting from a shortage of paved roads. Galoshes were worn nine months out of the year, and visitors automatically removed their shoes before entering another person's home.

In addition to physical discomfort, workers had to endure the loneliness and boredom of living in such remote areas as well as the suffocating atmosphere of security. Both sites were surrounded by barbed wire and armed guards, mail was censored and travel was limited. Except for a handful of scientists, none of the thousands who worked at Hanford and Oak Ridge knew what they were engaged in. They built huge buildings not knowing their purpose. They monitored dials not knowing what the dials were measuring. Only after the war did they learn they had been working to develop an atom bomb.

The work was excruciatingly slow. The massive plants produced only a few grams of the precious substances per day, and what was produced had to undergo extensive refinement. It

ODE TO MUD

To separate U-235 from U-238, a huge complex was built at Oak Ridge, Tennessee. Construction was an ongoing fact of life, and for a great part of the year the mostly unpaved roads were churned into mud by heavy vehicles. The mud was so pervasive that someone wrote this anonymous poem about it, found in *The Making of the Atomic Bomb* by Richard Rhodes.

In order not to check in late,
I've had to lose a lot of weight,
From swimming through a fair-sized flood
And wading through the goddam mud.

I've lost my rubbers and my shoes.
Perpetually I have the blues.
My spirits tumble with a thud
Because of all this goddam mud.

It's in my system so that when
I cut my finger now and then
Instead of bleeding just plain blood
Out pours a stream of goddam mud.

would be early 1945 before significant quantities of bomb-grade U-235 and plutonium would be ready.

OPPENHEIMER

In the meantime, a third site was selected for the research on and assembly of the bomb itself. The most important aspect of this decision was not the site but the man who would run it. Groves chose a man as opposite from himself as one could imagine, yet one whose ability and intellect he respected—J. Robert Oppenheimer.

Oppenheimer was known as one of the most brilliant theoretical physicists in the United States, but he had little experimental or administrative experience. He had breezed through Harvard in three years, then done graduate work in England and Germany. He returned to the United States in 1929 and accepted simultaneous teaching positions at Berkeley and the California Institute of Technology in Pasadena.

Oppenheimer's intellect was formidable. In addition to physics, he read classical French literature, taught himself Sanskrit (the ancient Hindu language), and had a deep interest in Oriental mysticism. His body was as frail as his mind was powerful. He had suffered from tuberculosis as a young man and, although six feet tall, never weighed more than 125 pounds. As a teenager, he spent some time recuperating at a ranch in the mountains near Santa Fe, New Mexico. In 1929, he and his brother bought a small ranch in the same area. He once wrote to a friend, "My two great loves are physics and desert country. It's a pity they can't be combined."[30] They eventually would be.

Oppenheimer was brought in to the atomic research picture in May 1942 as the director of research on fast neutron fission. He first met Groves in early October when the general came to Berkeley on an inspection tour. He told Groves that "a major change was called for in the work on the bomb itself. We needed a central laboratory devoted wholly to this purpose, where people could talk freely with each other."[31]

The complex at Oak Ridge, Tennessee, where U-235 was produced. Muddy conditions, tight security, and loneliness made life difficult at the site.

Despite the vast differences between the intellectual Oppenheimer and the bluff Groves, the general was impressed. "Why, Oppenheimer knows about everything," Groves said after the war. "He can talk to you about anything you bring up. Well, not exactly. I guess there are a few things he doesn't know about. He doesn't know anything about sports."[32]

Groves recommended Oppenheimer to head the bomb design and assembly, but there were problems. Oppenheimer had been involved in some left-wing causes in California in the 1930s, and his wife Kitty and a former fiancée had been members of the American Communist Party. The Military Policy Committee at first refused to make the appointment, but Groves persisted and finally had his way.

LOS ALAMOS

The first task facing this oddly paired couple was to find a site for the laboratory. For safety and security reasons, Groves wanted it to be as isolated as Oak Ridge and Hanford. One of the sites they inspected was Jemez Springs, New Mexico. Neither man liked it, but Oppenheimer, who knew the area well, remembered a nearby boys' school named for the cottonwood trees that abounded—Los Alamos.

The school sat atop a seven-thousand-foot mesa about twenty miles northwest of Santa Fe and seemed to be the ideal site, even including a view of Oppenheimer's beloved Sangre de Cristo Mountains. Soon, the school, along with an adjacent fifty thousand acres, most of it from the National Forest Service, was part of the Manhattan Project.

By the time the scientists, their families, and equipment began making their way up the rough, twisting road from Santa Fe to Los Alamos in March 1943, the quiet beauty of the mesa had been transformed. Construction crews were everywhere on unpaved streets among half-finished buildings. Housing was in short supply and, indeed, would always lag behind the number of people requiring it. Groves and Oppenheimer had envisioned a staff of a few dozen scientists and their families. By war's end, the population at Los Alamos, called "The Hill" by its inhabitants, was several thousand.

Among them, despite the crowding, isolation, and security restrictions, were many of the most brilliant minds in science. Early arrivals included Hans Bethe, Edward Teller, John von

Neumann, George Kistiakowski, Kenneth Bainbridge, and Emilio Segrè. They would later be joined by the likes of Fermi, Bohr, and Chadwick. As might be expected, these brilliant men were highly individualistic and resented any military-type discipline. It would take all of Oppenheimer's skill to act as an intermediary between the scientists and Groves, who called them "the largest collection of crackpots ever seen."[33]

LOS ALAMOS

Before Los Alamos was occupied by swarms of scientists and soldiers, the New Mexico mesa was occupied by the Los Alamos Ranch School for Boys. The school had been established in 1916 by Ashley Pond, a wealthy Detroit businessman who had fallen in love with New Mexico after recuperating from an illness there as a child.

Pond wanted to give other boys the same kind of experience. His school was to be modeled on the Boy Scouts of America, with a rigorous academic program matched by a rugged physical regimen. The boys wore uniforms modeled after the Boy Scouts. They started each day at 6:30 A.M. with exercises and breakfast. In addition to their academic courses, they had mandatory athletics, including horsemanship and camping.

Three boys practice the art of horsemanship at the Los Alamos Ranch School for Boys.

Enrollment was at a peak in the 1930s, with forty-five students plus the faculty and staff. The school boasted some distinguished graduates, including author Gore Vidal; Arthur Reed, president of Sears, Roebuck, and Company; Roy Chapin Jr., chairman of the board of American Motors Corporation; and John Crosby, founder and director of the Santa Fe Opera.

UNDER PRESSURE

These "crackpots," however, were under tremendous pressure to develop a practical military weapon in the shortest possible time. Guided mostly by theory (and backed up by little in the way of experimental results), they worked to design and build an atom bomb, to take the material produced by Oak Ridge and Hanford and turn theory into physical reality. From the earliest months, they irreverently referred to their end product, this terrible weapon of mass destruction, as "the gadget."

The basic problem to be solved was detonating the bomb—how to bring two segments of either U-235 or plutonium together to form a critical mass that would result in an explosion. In order for the bomb to be efficient—to obtain the maximum explosive force from a minimal amount of material—the segments had to be brought together quickly. Otherwise, the chain reaction would begin prematurely and energy would be lost. Also, the reaction needed to take place in a confined area, much like gunpowder that will explode when ignited within a bullet but will only flare up if loose and unconfined. The reactive material, therefore, had to be encased in a heavy material, the casing known as "tamper."

In addition, although the combined segments would fission spontaneously, Oppenheimer's team wanted a device—they called it an initiator—that would send an instantaneous spray of fast neutrons when the two segments of fissionable material were brought together. Finally, the entire assembly needed to be compact enough to fit inside an airplane and rigged so that it would detonate at the desired altitude.

Even before coming to Los Alamos, Oppenheimer, Teller, Bethe, and the others had been discussing how to design a bomb. They concluded that the best solution would be to have some sort of gun, or cannon, that would fire the two fissionable segments into each other at a velocity high enough to spark an instantaneous chain reaction. Some favored a design in which the two pieces would be fired simultaneously from either end of a barrel. They eventually decided, however, that it would be easier if one piece were placed at one end of a closed barrel and the other fired into it. The target piece would be a solid core with a hole bored into it. The shell would be a plug consisting of fissionable material and tamper that, when fired into the hole, would complete the assembly. This was the basic design of what came to be known as the "gun bomb."

OPPENHEIMER

Perhaps the most central figure in the development of the atom bomb was J. Robert Oppenheimer, director of the research facility at Los Alamos, New Mexico. Although he was an undeniably brilliant physicist, some people connected with the Manhattan Project questioned his ability as an administrator, citing his often brusque manner. He would surprise his critics by proving more than capable of managing and occasionally soothing the many large egos to be found at Los Alamos.

Oppenheimer was distinctive in appearance also. He almost always wore a porkpie hat, and he was rarely found without a pipe clenched in his teeth. Haakon Chevalier, a fellow professor at Berkeley, described him in this excerpt from *The Making of the Atomic Bomb* by Richard Rhodes.

> [Oppenheimer] was tall, nervous and intent, and he moved with an odd gait, a kind of jog, with a great deal of swinging of his limbs, his head always a little to one side, one shoulder higher than the other. But it was the head that was the most striking: the halo of wispy black curly hair, the fine, sharp nose, and especially the eyes, surprisingly blue, having a strange depth and intensity, and yet expressive of a candor that was altogether disarming. He looked like a young Einstein, and at the same time like an overgrown choir boy.

CRITICAL MASSES

By the spring of 1943, scientists had calculated the critical masses, the total amount of either U-235 or plutonium that, when suddenly brought together in a single mass, would result in a chain reaction. They found that about thirty-three pounds of U-235 would be required for a weapon or about eleven pounds of plutonium, which fissioned much more efficiently. Around this core, when assembled, would be a tamper of uranium weighing about one ton. The cannon would be seventeen feet long and weigh another five tons.

A young physicist at Los Alamos came up with a different idea. Seth Neddermeyer proposed that, instead of using explosives to

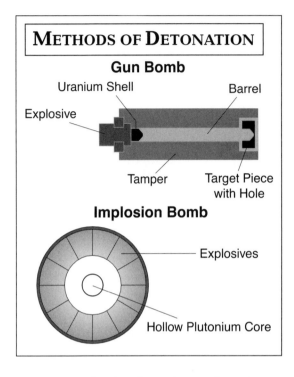

METHODS OF DETONATION

Gun Bomb

Uranium Shell

Barrel

Explosive

Tamper

Target Piece
with Hole

Implosion Bomb

Explosives

Hollow Plutonium Core

propel one segment against another, explosives should be packed around a hollow sphere of fissionable material. When detonated, the explosives would compress the material into a solid core—a critical mass. "This gun," said Neddermeyer referring to the cannon-type design, "will compress in one dimension. Two dimensions would be better. Three dimensions would be better still."[34]

Oppenheimer's reaction to the implosion idea was negative. How, he asked, could the impact of the explosive charges surrounding a sphere be made equal in all directions? Otherwise, it would be like squeezing a balloon filled with water and having it squirt out from between one's fingers. William "Deke" Parsons, a navy captain who was head of ordnance (artillery) research, was also discouraging. Neddermeyer's idea, he said, was like "whether he could blow in a beer can without splattering the beer."[35] Oppenheimer, nevertheless, maintained an open mind, allowing Neddermeyer to pursue his idea independently.

PROBLEM WITH PLUTONIUM

Meanwhile, Los Alamos scientists were discovering some unlooked-for and unwelcome properties of plutonium. Seaborg had shown—and others had since confirmed—that plutonium was preferable to U-235 as a bomb component. Plutonium had a greater cross-section, meaning that the structure of the nucleus presented a greater chance of fission when struck by a neutron.

Unfortunately, this also meant that a chain reaction might be started prematurely by a stray neutron in the split second before a critical mass was achieved. Just as unfortunately, plutonium (Pu-239) contained an impurity—the isotope Pu-240—that emitted stray neutrons. To eliminate this predetonation, the pieces of plutonium that, when joined, would fission would have to be brought together with a velocity beyond the capability of the gun design. Theoretically, however, Neddermeyer's implosion design would yield the velocity necessary for a plutonium bomb.

Reluctantly, Oppenheimer committed a massive research effort to the design of an implosion plutonium bomb. It would be radically different in shape and size from the uranium gun bomb. Whereas the latter, at this early stage, was seventeen feet long and two feet wide, the implosion bomb would be nine feet long and five feet wide, "a man-sized egg with tail fins."[36] The gun bomb was referred to in code as "Thin Man" and the implosion bomb as "Fat Man."

RECRUITING FOR LOS ALAMOS

Despite the importance of the atom bomb project, it was sometimes difficult for J. Robert Oppenheimer to recruit top scientists to come to Los Alamos. Eventually, however, the desire to be a part of history won out, as Oppenheimer recalled in Richard Rhodes's *The Making of the Atomic Bomb.*

> The prospect of coming to Los Alamos aroused great misgivings. It was to be a military post; men were asked to sign up more or less for the duration [of the war]; restrictions on travel and on the freedom of families to move about would be severe. . . . The notion of disappearing into the New Mexico desert for an indeterminate period and under quasi-military auspices disturbed a good many scientists, and the families of many more. But there was another side to it. Almost everyone realized that this was a great undertaking. Almost everyone knew that if it were completed successfully and rapidly enough, it might determine the outcome of the war. Almost everyone knew that it was an unparalleled opportunity to bring to bear the basic knowledge and art of science for the benefit of this country. Almost everyone knew that this job, if it were achieved, would be part of history. This sense of excitement, of devotion and of patriotism in the end prevailed.

Thin Man would soon get a new form and a new name. First, scientists realized in April 1943 that they had miscalculated the weight of the gun. They had based their estimates on army guns that were made for repeat firing. The gun used in the bomb would need to be fired only once. Instead of five tons it would weigh only one ton.

Then, in December, Segrè discovered that the fission rate of U-235 varied with altitude, because neutron activity from cosmic rays increased in the upper atmosphere. These stray neutrons caused spontaneous fission in U-235 and could lead to predetonation of a bomb. However, if the gun was shielded from cosmic rays, researchers found, less velocity was needed from the gun, so it could be shorter and lighter. The new design was only six feet long and was nicknamed "Little Boy."

By the end of 1943, many of the questions facing the Manhattan Project had been answered. U-235 and plutonium were being made at Oak Ridge and Hanford, although quantities were minute and better refining techniques were needed. And the basic design of the bombs had been determined, although much research was still needed, especially on implosion. Oppenheimer and Groves were convinced that they could make a working bomb, but only a full-scale test would prove them right.

4

TRINITY

At the start of 1944, the Manhattan Project was under increasing pressure to produce an atom bomb. Critics in Congress were questioning the tremendous expenditure—well over $1 billion. The military remained worried that Germany would develop nuclear weapons first. Oppenheimer and Groves, however, maintained that they had two workable designs—the U-235 gun and the plutonium implosion bomb—and could produce either or both in time to affect World War II. Much work still needed to be done, however, before theory could be made reality.

Part of Oppenheimer's task was to reconfigure the administrative structure at Los Alamos to reflect the new emphasis on the implosion bomb. He created two new divisions. Division G (for gadget) would study the physics of weapons and would be run by Robert Bacher, an early Oppenheimer recruit from the Massachusetts Institute of Technology. Division X (for explosives) would concentrate on making implosion work and would be directed by George Kistiakowski, a Harvard expert on explosives, assisted by Seth Neddermeyer and John von Neumann.

The new divisions were carved largely from Deke Parsons's ordnance division, and Parsons complained bitterly. Kistiakowski later wrote that the navy captain "was furious—he felt that I had by-passed him and that was outrageous. I can understand perfectly how he felt but I was a civilian, so was Oppie [Oppenheimer], and I didn't have to go through him."[37]

Parsons still had plenty of responsibility. The plutonium implosion bomb was an uncertainty. The uranium gun, Little Boy, while not yet a certainty, was considered the surest bet for an

In charge of the gun bomb, Deke Parsons complained bitterly when scientists and technicians were transferred from his division to two others that were developing the implosion bomb.

atomic weapon, and it was up to Parsons to finish the design and build it.

Considerable work on the gun bomb had already been done. Since September 1943, nearby Anchor Ranch had resounded with gunfire as various types of explosives were tested using naval anti-aircraft guns. Initially, the scientists were trying to achieve a muzzle velocity of three thousand feet per second, the speed thought necessary for a plutonium gun. When the presence of Pu-240 ruled out a plutonium gun, Parsons's task was made far easier. A muzzle velocity of two thousand feet per second would work for U-235, and the projected length of the gun could be reduced from seventeen to six feet with a corresponding reduction in weight.

EXPLOSIVE EXPERIMENTS

At Anchor Ranch, Parsons's group set up a test stand, firing shell after shell into a huge box of sand so that the pieces could be retrieved and studied. Eventually, cordite—an explosive commonly used in large gun ammunition—was chosen as the most efficient.

The gun design was simple—a three-inch barrel about six feet long. On one end—the target end—was a large piece of steel tamper surrounding concentric rings of U-235. The other end—the breech—held a primer that would ignite the cordite that, in turn, would propel the U-235 bullet into the target, which was shaped to receive it and thus initiate the chain reaction.

The gun design was the easy part. Figuring out exactly how much U-235 was necessary for a critical mass and whether forcing two halves of that mass together would produce the desired explosion was much more difficult.

The first answer came from Enrico Fermi, whose team was known as the Water Boiler Group. It boiled water, certainly, but with atomic reactors instead of ordinary heat. The group took its name because the cold water pumped into the reactors as a coolant was boiling after passing through. Fermi was able to bombard a tiny sample of U-235 with fast neutrons. After measuring the fission that occurred, the amount of U-235 necessary for a bomb was calculated at about thirty-three pounds.

The calculation of U-235's critical mass was both good news and bad news. In January 1945, the Oak Ridge plant was capable of producing about seven ounces of bomb-grade U-235 per day. That would mean that enough would be available for a weapon by midyear, but it would also mean there would be no full-scale test. There simply was not enough U-235.

This left the problem of how to test whether or not the calculated amount would actually result in an explosion. The solution was found by Otto Frisch, who with his aunt Lise Meitner had first explained how fission takes place. He reasoned that if a critical mass could be assembled only for a split second, it could be measured to determine the amount of energy released without the threat of an explosion. His idea was to compile a quantity of a uranium compound sufficient to make a critical mass except it would have a hole in the middle. Through this hole a piece of the material would be dropped, thus creating—for a fraction of a second—a chain reaction.

THE DRAGON'S TAIL

When Frisch explained his experiment to an associate, Richard Feynman, Feynman laughed and said it would be like tickling a sleeping dragon's tail. The name stuck, and the Dragon's Tail experiment proceeded in February 1945.

Frisch's group worked alongside Fermi's in a remote site known as Omega Canyon. The experiments there were considered so dangerous that they had been deliberately placed far away from the main Los Alamos technical area. The dragon consisted of a ten-foot iron frame nicknamed the "guillotine" through which four aluminum guide rails passed. The scientists stacked blocks of uranium hydride around the rails, just one block short of enough to start a chain reaction. The missing block, about two by six inches, was placed within the runners and allowed to drop through the middle of the pile below.

As Frisch later wrote,

It was as near as we could possibly go towards starting an atomic explosion without actually being blown up, and the results were most satisfactory. Everything happened exactly as it should. When the core was dropped through the hole we got a large burst of neutrons and a temperature rise of several degrees in that very short split second during which the chain reaction proceeded as a sort of stifled explosion. We worked under great pressure because the material had to be returned [to Oak Ridge] by a certain date to be made into [U-235] metal.[38]

By April, enough enriched, or bomb-grade, U-235 was available for Frisch to make similar experiments on the metal itself rather than on a compound. These experiments confirmed the dragon's results. The U-235 was now ready to be fashioned into the

MEDICINE AT LOS ALAMOS

The isolation of the scientists and their families at Los Alamos brought about some unusual problems for the military doctors. Few of them were obstetricians or pediatricians, yet the birth rate at Los Alamos was very high. It was so high, in fact, that at one point General Leslie Groves considered trying to order people not to have children until J. Robert Oppenheimer talked him out of it.

There was also a great need for psychiatrists because of the tremendous stress the scientists were under. Laura Fermi, wife of physicist Enrico Fermi, as quoted in Richard Rhodes's *The Making of the Atomic Bomb*, described the doctors' plight.

They had prepared for the emergencies of the battlefields, and they were faced instead with a high-strung bunch of men, women, and children. High-strung because altitude affected us, because our men worked long hours under unrelenting pressure; high-strung because we were too many of a kind, too close to one another, too unavoidable even during relaxation hours, and we were all (as Groves had warned his officers not

two components that would go into Little Boy's gun. The cost of
producing those few pounds of metal had been almost $1 billion.

Oppenheimer, Groves, and the rest of the Los Alamos team
were convinced that Little Boy would work. They did not have
such an optimistic outlook for Fat Man, the implosion plutonium
bomb, however. Ever since it had been proposed by Seth Neddermeyer early in 1943, few thought it was a workable design.
Theoretical research by John von Neumann, however, showed
that the idea had possibilities, and Oppenheimer assigned Neddermeyer to pursue it.

THE BEER CAN EXPERIMENT

Neddermeyer began his series of experiments on July 4, 1943,
planting explosive charges around hollow steel pipes in what
Parsons derisively called the beer can experiment. The experiments produced few results, but it hardly mattered—at the time.

entirely tongue-in-cheek) crackpots; high-strung because we
felt powerless under strange circumstances, irked by minor
annoyances that we blamed on the Army and that drove us to
unreasonable and pointless rebellion.

*Psychiatrists were in great demand at Los Alamos due to the pres-
sure of working in close quarters such as these laboratories.*

The Los Alamos team was confident that Little Boy (top) would work, but there were doubts about Fat Man (bottom).

After all, implosion was considered a sideshow. The gun bomb design, both for U-235 and plutonium, was the main event.

In early 1944, however, it was becoming increasingly evident that implosion might be the best, and perhaps only, bet for a plutonium bomb. Oppenheimer and Groves decided Neddermeyer needed help and brought in Kistiakowski. Neddermeyer resented the newcomer and, although the two agreed to work together, results remained disappointing. Finally, in June, Oppenheimer placed Kistiakowski in charge of the implosion project, a move that embittered Neddermeyer.

The project began to make progress in the first half of the year, helped mightily by an infusion of scientists from Great Britain who had decided to suspend their own research and join the American team. One, James L. Tuck, provided a crucial bit of insight. The basic problem was that explosions produced shock waves that bulged outward. A series of these shock waves converging on a sphere would not produce the uniform pressure needed to compress the plutonium core.

In Britain, Tuck had done extensive work on shells designed to pierce armor. These explosive charges were shaped so that, instead of expanding outward, the shock wave was focused into a jet. Tuck suggested that similar specially shaped charges, called "lenses" since they would focus explosions much like an optical lens focuses light, could be arranged to provide an even pressure.

Arriving at the proper composition of the explosive charges, the proper shape, and the proper arrangement was a long process of trial and error. The once-tranquil Anchor Ranch sounded like a battlefield as thousands of lens casings using tons of explosives—up to fifty tons in a single month—were detonated.

Progress was slow, and Oppenheimer decided that a full-scale test of Fat Man would eventually be necessary. Groves reluctantly

Up to fifty tons of explosives a month were used in order to determine the proper composition, shape, and arrangement of the charges for the implosion bomb.

agreed. Earlier in the year he had promised Vannevar Bush and James Conant in Washington that a bomb would be ready by the end of 1944. He now revised his estimate to mid-1945.

THE STUDY OF EXPLOSIVES

Part of the problem was that few physicists had studied explosives to the extent necessary for an implosion bomb. To do so, they first had to develop instruments to measure and chart the shock waves. X rays worked well in the study of the explosive charges. As the shock wave expanded, the density of the charge changed, and the change was recorded by rapidly pulsating X rays that produced a sequence of images similar to a movie film.

The dense metal core was harder to study, and scientists tried several methods. Models were placed in magnetic fields to chart the explosive shock waves. Electric wires were inserted in the core at precise levels to record the velocity of the charge at various points. A device known as a betatron fired pulsed X rays through implosion models into a cloud chamber, where their tracks could be photographed. The final method was to put a source of gamma rays, radioactive lanthanum, within the core and measure the patterns of radioactivity during the explosion.

This last technique was extremely dangerous because of the intensity of the gamma radiation. When it was first used, no one knew how much radiation would be released, so Kistiakowski and fellow physicist Luis Alvarez watched from tanks borrowed from the U.S. Army. Alvarez later wrote,

> I was sitting in the tank when the explosion went off. George Kistiakowski was in one tank and I was in the other. We were looking through the periscopes and all that happened was that it blew a lot of dust in our eyes. And then—we hadn't thought about this possibility at all—the whole forest around us caught fire. These pieces of white hot metal went flying off into the wild blue yonder setting trees on fire. We were almost surrounded.[39]

After months of laborious testing, Kistiakowski's team settled on a design by Neumann. The charges were shaped like pyramids with the tops cut off, the smaller ends pointing inward toward the core. Inside each charge was a cone of "slow" explosives surrounded by "fast" explosives. The fast explosives were detonated first, with the shock wave bulging inward until it reached the slow explosives. The slow explosives slowed the shock wave in the center, allowing the curve to change shape to fit the spherical core. Careful placement of the charges enabled a symmetrical shock wave to act on the core, compressing it to half its original size.

THE INITIATOR

The final problem to be solved was at the center of the core rather than around the sphere. The critical mass of plutonium needed an instant source of neutrons to ensure that the chain reaction took place. This was the job of the initiator. Hans Bethe and a team worked for a year to perfect a design about the size of a golf ball that had polonium and beryllium separated by layers of foil. When the core was imploded, the two elements would be crushed together, allowing the alpha particles emitted by the radioactive polonium to knock neutrons from the beryllium nuclei and start the chain reaction.

THE SCIENTIFIC APPROACH

Some of the scientists at Los Alamos applied their craft even to modes of relaxation. One of the most popular forms of recreation was square dancing, and noted scholars who hailed from Hungary, Germany, the Soviet Union, Great Britain, Sweden, and Italy showed they could do-si-do with the best of them.

One who was hesitant to join in the dancing was Enrico Fermi. Although his wife and daughter tried to entice him onto the dance floor, he waited and watched, memorizing the various steps. When he considered himself prepared, he asked one of the leading dancers, Bernice Brode, to be his partner. She recalled the incident in *The Making of the Atomic Bomb* by Richard Rhodes.

He offered to be the head couple, which I thought most unwise for his first venture, but I couldn't do anything about it and the music began. He led me out on the exact beat, knew exactly each move to make and when. He never made a mistake, then or thereafter, but I wouldn't say he enjoyed himself. . . . He [danced] with his brains instead of his feet.

By November 1944 the war in Europe was reaching an end. Allied troops had landed in France in June and were rapidly advancing on Germany. The war in the Pacific was also going well for the Allies, but an enormous hurdle—the invasion of mainland Japan—still remained. If the atom bomb were to help end the war, it needed to be soon. In March 1945, Oppenheimer agreed to freeze weapons design and concentrate on two tasks—building a Little Boy for use against Japan and preparing for the test of Fat Man.

The code name for the test, Trinity, had been selected by Oppenheimer. His inspiration was a poem, one in the collection *Holy Sonnets* by Englishman John Donne, that referred to the Holy Trinity—Father, Son, and Holy Spirit—and had destruction as its principal theme.

The site for Trinity had been carefully selected by Kenneth Bainbridge, head of the High Explosives Group. He wanted a site that was flat, remote, within reasonable distance of Los Alamos, and had good weather. He considered sites in Colorado, Utah, and Texas before recommending a section eighteen miles by twenty-four miles in the northwest sector of the Alamogordo Bombing Range in the desolate Jornada del Muerto area of New Mexico about 150 miles south of Los Alamos.

JUMBO

General Groves had initially been opposed to a test. He was afraid that, if the bomb failed, precious plutonium would be scattered and lost. To prevent this, Bainbridge and Kistiakowski considered several alternatives, including exploding the bomb in water, underground, or in a large container. Only after this last option was approved did Groves agree to a test. A huge steel container nicknamed "Jumbo" was built, but eventually discarded. Kistiakowski finally convinced Groves that exploding Fat Man inside Jumbo would make it impossible to measure how effective the bomb was.

Work began on the Trinity site in November 1944. The spot where the bomb was to be detonated was called ground zero. Observation posts were placed ten thousand yards to the north, west, and south, a distance that the scientists had calculated—and that they hoped—would be safe. The base camp consisting of laboratories, dormitories, and a dining hall was about ten miles away. Since Trinity was to be only a temporary facility,

To prevent the loss of plutonium if Fat Man failed to explode properly, a huge steel container nicknamed "Jumbo" (pictured) was built. Because it would make measuring the bomb's power impossible, Jumbo was later discarded.

Groves spent as little money on comforts as possible. Only reluctantly, for instance, did he agree to spend $5,000 to have the roads paved, and then only because the scientists complained that the dust might harm electrical components.

Security at Trinity was as tight as Groves could make it. Anyone driving from Los Alamos to Trinity was forbidden from stopping anywhere south of Albuquerque except for a single restaurant where (it was rumored) Groves had a security agent working as the cook. The site itself was under heavy guard by army troops, who passed the long, boring hours by shooting at antelope.

Perhaps envisioning the biggest firecracker ever, Oppenheimer and Bainbridge initially scheduled the test for July 4, 1945. Delays in the shipment of plutonium from Hanford and the shipment of molds for the explosive lenses, however, forced them to reconsider. The Cowpuncher Committee, so-called because it was supposed to ride herd on the many aspects of the test, decided that July 13 was the earliest possible date.

Meteorologist John Huber had the large and largely thankless job of trying to tell Groves when the weather would be favorable. His first choice was July 18–19. July 20–21 and July 14 would be acceptable, he said, and July 16 was his third choice. Groves chose July 16. Harry S. Truman, who had become president after Roosevelt's death in April, would be at a conference with the leaders of Great Britain and the Soviet Union in July and August and wanted assurance that the bomb worked before negotiating with the Soviets.

SPREADING THE WORD

As the date grew closer, the pace of activity sped up. From across the country the scientists who had been part of the Manhattan Project began to make their way to New Mexico. Using prearranged wording, Oppenheimer sent coded telegrams to Ernest Lawrence at Berkeley and Arthur Compton at Chicago reading, "Any time after the 15th would be a good time for our fishing trip. Because we are not certain of the weather we may be delayed several days. As we do not have enough sleeping bags to go around, we ask you please do not bring anyone with you."[40]

One of the problems was that Oppenheimer had insisted on testing a copy of Fat Man that would contain a sphere of explosive lenses without the plutonium core. The most perfect blocks—sixty-four of them—had been carefully chosen at Los Alamos and set aside for Trinity. Now, Teller raced to prepare sixty-four more, some of which contained air bubbles that had been revealed by X rays. Working by himself at night because of the danger of an explosion, Teller used a dental drill to reach the air pockets and then poured molten explosives through the holes to fill the pockets. He later wrote that he wasn't nervous during the process: "You don't worry about it. I mean, if fifty pounds of explosives goes in your lap, you won't know it."[41]

DEATH AT LOS ALAMOS

Despite the fact that they were working with some of the deadliest substances on earth, the workforce at Los Alamos suffered only two deaths as a direct result of exposure to radiation. The first occurred in August 1945, a month after the first atomic test. Harry Daghlian, a young physicist, was assembling small bricks of uranium into an arrangement that was supposed to be just short of a critical mass. Just as the arrangement reached that point, a brick slipped and fell into the middle of the pile.

Daghlian immediately pushed the brick off with his hand, but not before he was enveloped in a blue glow of gamma radiation. He soon developed second-degree burns on his hands, face, and abdomen and died twenty-eight days later.

Less than a year later, Louis Slotin was lowering one hemisphere of beryllium onto another to form a sphere that would, should they touch, constitute a critical mass. They were supposed to be prevented from touching by a screwdriver inserted between them, but the screwdriver slipped. The same blue glow burst forth, and Slotin was dead in nine days.

THE TRIP TO TRINITY

On Thursday, July 12, the plutonium core, resting in a specially padded case on the backseat of an army car, was driven from Los Alamos to Trinity. It was carried carefully to an old ranch house and surrounded with guards. The outer sphere with its explosive charges started its journey just after midnight on Friday the 13th. The metal sphere had a special section on top that could be opened for the insertion of the "plug," the plutonium core and initiator.

That afternoon, under the broiling desert sun, Fat Man was assembled directly beneath the trap door of the shed atop the one-hundred-foot tower at ground zero. When Robert Bacher and his Gadget Group started to lower the cylindrical plug into the sphere, however, they found it wouldn't fit. "Imagine our consternation when . . . it would not enter!" wrote team member Bryce McDaniel. "Dismayed, we halted our efforts in order not to damage the pieces and stopped to think about it. Could we have made a mistake?"[42]

No, they had not, and Bacher saw why. The two pieces fit together so closely that the slight expansion of the plug inside the hot ranch house prevented it from sliding into its proper place. Bacher suggested the team wait a few minutes and try again. When they did, the plug went smoothly into the interior of the sphere.

FINAL PREPARATIONS

On Saturday morning, Fat Man was slowly lifted into place. Tape to keep out dust covered the spots where detonators would be attached to the explosive lenses. When the bomb was in place, the meticulous job of attaching the detonators and checking the hundreds of electrical connections began. Oppenheimer, his weight down to 115 pounds from the effects of stress, fretted over his creation like a mother hen, darting from place to place and making everyone around him nervous.

Oppenheimer's mood was not brightened when word came from Los Alamos that the test of the nonnuclear copy of Fat Man had not produced the desired results. He lashed out at Kistiakowski, blaming him for what he now thought would be a failure of the primary test. Finally, Kistiakowski, having endured enough verbal abuse, simply got up and left. He later wrote, "I just couldn't take it any more, just went out into the desert."[43]

About 4 o'clock on Sunday afternoon, only twelve hours before the test, Oppenheimer climbed alone to the top of the tower to make one last check. The wind had increased, and there was a distant sound of thunder. A storm was approaching, and tempers began to match the weather. Soon after he came down, Groves arrived and began demanding better weather forecasts from the beleaguered Huber, who protested that he had favored other dates and that it had been Groves who picked the 16th. He told the general that the storm should die down before dawn. "You'd better be right on this," Groves said, "or I'm going to hang you."[44] No one would get much sleep that Sunday night.

ZERO HOUR

Finally, the storm passed and the fateful time arrived. When the firing circuit closed at 5:29:45 A.M. the detonators fired, igniting the explosive lenses. The shock waves bulged, encountered the slow explosives, turned inside out, and slammed into the uranium tamper. The plutonium core, about the size of a grapefruit, was squeezed to the size of a golf ball. The initiator was crushed inward, and the beryllium neutrons thus freed smashed into the plutonium nuclei. Within a tiny fraction of a second, millions more nuclei were shattered, creating temperatures and pressures comparable to the center of the sun.

After the briefest of instants, the energy radiated outwards and a false dawn lit the desert sky. Fat Man, the plutonium bomb, worked. Soon, it would be the turn of Fat Man's cousin, Little Boy, but there would be no preliminary test. At about

ALWAYS THE SCIENTIST

When the world's first atom bomb was detonated on July 16, 1945, at the Trinity site in New Mexico, those who had helped make it possible had varied reactions. Some laughed and cheered. Others prayed. Others were simply thoughtful, realizing the enormity of what they had done.

One man, though, Italian-born Enrico Fermi, couldn't resist his scientist's urge to experiment. Fermi, who in 1942 had overseen the world's first controlled chain reaction at the University of Chicago, had been one of several senior physicists to place bets on the force of the explosion. Without waiting for instruments to tell him what that force was, he decided to find out for himself, as he described in a typed document pictured in *The Day the Sun Rose Twice* by Ferenc Morton Szasz.

> About 40 seconds after the explosion the air blast reached me. I tried to estimate its strength by dropping from about six feet small pieces of paper before, during and after the passage of the blast wave. Since at the time there was no wind I could observe very distinctly and actually measure the displacement of the pieces of paper that were in the process of falling while the blast was passing. The shift was about 2-½ meters, which, at the time, I estimated to correspond to the blast that would be produced by ten thousand tons of T.N.T.

Fermi's calculations were a little bit off. The size of the blast was actually closer to twenty thousand tons of TNT.

Fat Man detonates successfully on the morning of July 16, 1945 (top). After the explosion, Oppenheimer and Groves stand next to the remains of the one-hundred-foot tower.

the same time that Oppenheimer murmured the line from the Bhagavad Gita about becoming the "shatterer of worlds," two sailors carried a lead bucket aboard the USS *Indianapolis* docked in San Francisco Bay. In the bucket was Little Boy's U-235 bullet. It was bound for the Pacific island of Tinian and from there—in just a few days—to the skies over Japan.

PIKA-DON

Design and manufacture may have been the primary problems facing the leaders of the U.S. atom bomb project, but there were other issues to be settled as well. If bombs could be built, how would they be delivered to their targets? What would those targets be? Indeed, should the bomb be dropped at all? If so, should it be dropped only as a warning or in such a way as to cause maximum death and destruction? The answers to these questions were revealed in a four-day span in August 1945 as the horrors of nuclear war were unleashed on Japan.

THE SUPERFORTRESS

As far back as June 1943, physicists had contacted the U.S. Army Air Corps, as the Air Force was then known, to see what planes were capable of carrying a seventeen-foot-long device in the bomb bay. There was only one, the British Lancaster, but the Americans were unwilling to have their invention delivered by a non-American plane. Fortunately, there was an airplane on the drawing board that, with some modification, would serve— the B-29. Nicknamed the Superfortress, the B-29 was the first true intercontinental bomber, designed to fly up to four thousand miles and carry a bomb load of up to two hundred tons. It was also the first pressurized bomber able to cruise at altitudes above the range of antiaircraft fire and most fighter aircraft.

The atom bomb posed two problems for the B-29: length and weight. Designers solved the weight problem by strengthening the mechanism inside the plane that would release the bomb. The length problem largely disappeared when design improvements reduced the length of the bomb to less than ten feet. In

August 1944 seventeen modified B-29s were ordered to be built at the Martin Aircraft Plant in Omaha, Nebraska.

That same month, the Air Corps began to assemble and train special crews that would fly the mission. The man chosen to command these crews was Lieutenant Colonel Paul W. Tibbets, a twenty-nine-year-old veteran of the European war. Tibbets, who had served as a test pilot for the B-29, reported for duty to Major General Uzal Ent, commander of the Second Air Force. Concerning the new weapon, Ent told him,

> We don't know anything about it yet. We don't know what it can do. . . . You've got to mate it to the airplane and determine the tactics, the training, and the ballistics—everything. These are all parts of your problem. This thing is going to be very big. I believe it has the potential and the possibility of ending the war.[45]

Seen from the cockpit of another B-29, two Superfortresses drop their bombs on a Japanese target. Seventeen modified B-29s were ordered for use by the Manhattan Project.

DROPPING PUMPKINS

The new unit was designated the 509th Composite Group, and Tibbets chose Wendover Field in Utah as a training site. The new B-29s began arriving in October. There, above the desert, Tibbets and his crews practiced dropping dummy bombs—nicknamed pumpkins for their bright orange color—from thirty thousand feet. The pilots were taught to execute a quick getaway maneuver after the drop, sending their planes into a sharp diving turn. From this, they guessed that the explosion would be enormous, but only Tibbets and a handful of senior officers knew the destructive power of what the B-29s would carry.

The next spring, the military began looking for a suitable site to base the 509th, a place from which it could launch a mission against Japan. The choice was the island of Tinian, a thirty-eight-square-mile chunk of volcanic rock in the Mariana Islands, about fifteen hundred miles from Tokyo. Tinian had been captured the previous summer at a cost of almost seven thousand Japanese and American lives. Now, the one-time tropical paradise had become a huge airport. The coral had been leveled, and six 2-mile-long concrete runways had been constructed for the B-29s that were pounding Japanese cities. One observer said, "From the air this island, smaller than Manhattan, looked like a giant aircraft carrier, its deck loaded with bombers."[46] As the scientists at Los Alamos worked to perfect Fat Man and Little Boy, U.S. Navy construction crews—the Seabees—on Tinian were building the special facilities that would enable the bombs to be loaded into Tibbets's B-29s.

At the same time, in the United States, military and political leaders were discussing where, and even if, the atom bomb should be dropped. The man who had the ultimate responsibility for this decision had only just learned of its existence. On April 13, 1945, the day after President Franklin Roosevelt died, his successor, Harry Truman, was told about the Manhattan Project, about which he had been kept totally uninformed. Truman was briefed by Secretary of War Henry Stimson, who told him, "Within four months we shall in all probability have completed the most terrible weapon ever known in human history, one bomb of which could destroy a whole city."[47]

Lieutenant Colonel Paul W. Tibbets was chosen to command the special crews that would fly the first atomic missions.

THE INTERIM COMMITTEE

Two weeks later Truman appointed what he named the Interim Committee to make recommendations about the present and future use of the atom bomb. Included on the committee were Stimson, Vannevar Bush, James Conant, Ernest Lawrence, Fermi, Oppenheimer, and, as Truman's special representative, the new secretary of state, James Byrnes.

The Interim Committee's discussions focused on two issues, one military, the other political. The military decision was how to use the bomb to bring the war to a quick conclusion. The war in Europe was over, Nazi leader Adolf Hitler having committed suicide in his bunker underneath Berlin on April 30. The Pacific conflict, however, was dragging on, and many military leaders thought that only an invasion of the Japanese mainland would bring it to an end. They had set a tentative date of November 1, 1945, for the invasion, which was projected to last up to a year and to cost hundreds of thousands of American lives. "Japanese are a fanatical people," a former ambassador to Tokyo told Truman, "and are capable of fighting to the last ditch and the last man."[48]

The committee discussed the possibility of exploding the bomb over an uninhabited area as a warning to the Japanese, calling on them to surrender or have it be used on their cities. Stimson held this view, but he was in the minority. Oppen-

President Harry Truman (pictured) was told about the Manhattan Project the day after President Franklin Roosevelt died.

heimer was sympathetic but was doubtful that such a warning would work:

> You ask yourself would the Japanese government as then constituted and with divisions between the peace party and the war party, would it have been influenced by an enormous nuclear firecracker detonated at a great height doing little damage and your answer is as good as mine. I don't know.[49]

DEMONSTRATION OR DESTRUCTION?

Once the Trinity test had proved that the atomic bomb worked and was capable of mass destruction, the debate within the political, scientific, and military segments of the Manhattan Project was how to use it. Many people shied away from dropping the bomb on a Japanese city, fully aware of the number of people who would be killed. Instead, they thought that perhaps a demonstration of the bomb's power would convince the Japanese to surrender.

Shortly after the Trinity test, a committee consisting of J. Robert Oppenheimer, Ernest Lawrence, Arthur Compton, and Enrico Fermi met to discuss whether an effective enough demonstration explosion could be arranged. In its recommendation, this excerpt of which is found in *The Making of the Atomic Bomb* by Richard Rhodes, the committee recognized

> our obligation to our nation to use the weapons to help save American lives in the Japanese war. . . . Those who advocate a purely technical demonstration would wish to outlaw the use of atomic weapons, and have feared that if we use the weapons now our position in future negotiations would be prejudiced. Others emphasize the opportunity of saving American lives by immediate military use, and believe that such use will improve the international prospects, in that they are more concerned with the prevention of war than the elimination of this specific weapon. We find ourselves closer to these latter views; we can propose no technical demonstration likely to bring an end to the war; we see no acceptable alternative to direct military use.

Byrnes added that such a warning blast might only serve to give the Japanese time to move thousands of American prisoners of war into their cities as human shields.

The other consideration was political and involved the Soviet Union, which had never declared war on Japan and had swallowed up much of Eastern Europe in violation of agreements between the Allies. The alliance among the United States, Great Britain, and the Soviet Union had been an uneasy one from the start. The Americans and British distrusted the Soviets and were distrusted in return. Now, the Americans were afraid that the Soviets would wait until Japan was almost defeated, then come into the war and do in Asia what they had done in Eastern Europe. Byrnes especially argued that the bomb ought to be used quickly and forcefully so that "Japan will surrender and Russia will not get in so much on the kill."[50]

On June 1, the Interim Committee recommended to Truman that the bomb should be used against Japan, as soon as possible, on targets to be decided by the military. Truman agreed.

THE TARGET COMMITTEE

Stimson also had appointed a separate Target Committee, which first met on April 15, two days after Truman had been briefed on the Manhattan Project. In addition to the chair, Brigadier General Thomas Farrell, there were two Air Corps officers and five scientists. Their task was to recommend no more than four Japanese targets, each one an urban or industrial area. Groves had instructed Farrell to select targets "which would most adversely affect the will of the Japanese people to continue the war. Beyond that, they should be military in nature."[51] Ideally, Groves said, the targets should not have already undergone extensive bombing.

This last stipulation ruled out Tokyo, which had been pounded for months by B-29s carrying conventional bombs. Even so, the Target Committee studied seventeen cities, Tokyo among them. Weather conditions were studied, and calculations made concerning blast damage and probable casualties. Finally, the committee recommended four targets: Kyoto, Hiroshima, Yokohama, and Kokura.

The committee met again in May, this time with Tibbets. After discussion, the three main targets were Kyoto, Hiroshima, and Niigata. Stimson, however, did not want Kyoto bombed. The ancient city was the center of Japanese culture and religion, and Stimson thought it would be barbaric to destroy it, preferring a more military target instead. Accordingly, the committee settled on Hiroshima, Kokura, and Niigata in that order of importance. Among the secondary targets was the port city of Nagasaki.

On July 24 Groves drafted the order for the use of the atom bomb. It went through the chain of command all the way to Stimson and Chief of Staff General George Marshall, who were with Truman at his conference with Winston Churchill and Joseph Stalin in the Berlin suburb of Potsdam. Presumably, they showed the order to Truman, although there is no record.

Because of the long-standing cooperation of American and British scientists, Churchill knew about the atom bomb. When Truman informed Stalin, the Soviet leader simply said he hoped it would be used to good effect against the Japanese. The Soviets no doubt knew much about the Manhattan Project as a result of espionage at Los Alamos, but they probably did not understand how destructive such a bomb would be.

Winston Churchill, Truman, and Joseph Stalin shake hands at the Potsdam Conference in July, 1945. When informed about the bomb, Stalin simply said he hoped that it would be put to good use against the Japanese.

THE POTSDAM DECLARATION

On July 26, the United States, Great Britain, and China issued the Potsdam Declaration. The Soviet Union, not at war with Japan, had not signed, nor had Byrnes wanted it to. He was afraid that Stalin would demand too much in return for his signature. No doubt with the atom bomb in mind, the declaration called on Japan to surrender immediately or face "prompt and utter destruction."[52]

Although there was a growing desire among many prominent Japanese to seek a negotiated peace, the military party still ruled. On July 28, Prime Minister Kantaro Suzuki rejected the Potsdam Declaration, saying it should be *mokusatusu,* or treated with contempt. Stimson later wrote, "In the face of this rejection we could only proceed to demonstrate that the ultimatum had meant exactly what it had said. . . . For such a purpose the atomic bomb was an imminently suitable weapon."[53] Plans for dropping of the bomb thus went forward.

Tibbets and his crews had been on Tinian since June. After training in Utah, they had practiced overwater approaches near Cuba and now had eleven B-29s specially modified for atom bombs. The engines were more reliable than previous models, with fuel injectors replacing carburetors. The bomb bay was enlarged to accommodate Fat Man. As they waited for orders, the crews kept their skills honed, flying dummy runs from Tinian to Iwo Jima and back.

On July 26, the same day of the Potsdam Declaration, the USS *Indianapolis* had arrived at Tinian with Little Boy's uranium bullet. At the same time, pieces of the target assembly were flown from the United States along with the plutonium core and initiator of a second Fat Man. Five days later, Little Boy was assembled, complete except for the cordite explosives that would be installed onboard the airplane en route to Japan.

Now, everything hinged on the weather. Groves's order had said the mission could be flown any time after August 1. On that day, however, a typhoon was approaching Japan, and Tibbets had to wait. Three days later, the forecast was for clear weather over Japan. The go-ahead was given for the mission to be carried out on August 6.

Tibbets had briefed his crews on August 4. This mission, he told them, was the most important they had ever flown, probably the most important in the war. They were forbidden

On July 26 the USS Indianapolis *arrived at Tinian Island with Little Boy's uranium bullet.*

to write letters home or even to talk about the mission among themselves.

LOADING LITTLE BOY

On the afternoon of August 5, Little Boy was covered with a tarp and transported from the assembly shed to a special loading pit under the airplane that would carry it. The new B-29 had never been named. Tibbets, who would pilot it, chose his mother's given names and sought out a painter to put the name on the nose in four-foot-high letters—Enola Gay.

Little Boy would be detonated at a predetermined height— nineteen hundred feet—above the target, Hiroshima. The firing mechanism consisted of four radar units known as Archies, which would bounce their signals against the ground. When at least two of the four units confirmed the proper altitude, a charge would be sent to primers that would ignite the cordite, driving the uranium bullet into its target component.

The crews—there would be a spotter plane and two observer planes—ate breakfast at midnight. In addition to Tibbets, there would be eleven other men aboard the *Enola Gay.* The copilot was Captain Robert Lewis; the bombardier, Major Robert

Farebee. The man who would make the final preparations for Little Boy would be Deke Parsons, who had contributed so much to its development.

The *Enola Gay* took off at 2:45 A.M. on August 6. Fifteen minutes later, Parsons got to work in the cramped bomb bay. He removed a plate at the rear of the bomb, carefully inserted the four cordite charges, replaced the plate, and connected the firing line. Almost all there was to do now was wait.

The flight would take about five hours. Only a few of the crewmen slept. One, tail gunner Robert Caron, asked Tibbets what exactly it was the *Enola Gay* was carrying. Tibbets was evasive. Caron asked him, "Colonel, are we splitting atoms today?" Tibbets replied, "That's about it."[54]

FINAL BRIEFING

On the afternoon of August 4, 1945, Lieutenant Colonel Paul Tibbets briefed the crews who would fly the mission from the Pacific island of Tinian to drop the atom bomb on Hiroshima, Japan. One of the crew members, Abe Spitzer, violated the strict security rules and kept a diary of his experiences. As quoted in *Enola Gay* by Gordon Thomas and Max Morgan Witts, Spitzer gave this summary of Tibbets's final words.

> The colonel began by saying that whatever any of us, including himself, had done before was small potatoes compared to what we were going to do now. Then he said the usual things, but he said them well, as if he meant them, about how proud he was to have been associated with us, about how high our morale had been, and how difficult it was not knowing what we were doing, thinking maybe we were wasting our time and that the "gimmick" was just somebody's wild dream. He was personally honored and he was sure all of us were, to have been chosen to take part in this raid, which he said—and all the other big-wigs nodded when he said it—would shorten the war by at least six months. And you got the feeling that he really thought this bomb would end the war, period.

The Enola Gay *sits at the airfield on Tinian prior to the mission. Tibbets named the plane after his mother.*

At 7:30 A.M. Parsons completed the final arming of Little Boy. The scout plane reported good weather ahead. The *Enola Gay* climbed to its bombing altitude of thirty-one thousand feet. When it was twelve miles from the target, Major Farebee took control of the plane, flying it through the bombsight. His target was a bridge across the Ota River in central Hiroshima. Farebee made some final course corrections and released the bomb.

HELL AT HIROSHIMA

Forty-three seconds later, Little Boy exploded over Hiroshima. The *Enola Gay*, heeled over sharply, was by this time eleven miles away. Still, the shock wave tossed the B-29 about like a toy. Caron, from his vantage point in the rear, could see Hiroshima:

> The mushroom [cloud] was a spectacular sight, a bubbling mass of purple-gray smoke and you could see it had a red core in it and everything was burning inside. . . . I saw fires spring up in different places, like flames shooting up on a bed of coals. . . . I can still see it—that mushroom and that turbulent mass—it looked like lava or molasses covering the whole city.[55]

Beneath that mushroom cloud was a hell on earth.

THE KILLING ZONE

Within an instant after the blast, the air temperature within half a mile of ground zero rose to fifty-four hundred degrees Fahrenheit. Virtually all the people exposed within that circle were reduced to charred, blackened lumps, all the liquid parts of their bodies having instantly boiled away.

Those killed instantly were in many ways the lucky ones. Farther from the center, the people fell victim to *pika-don*, Japanese for "flash-boom." Those unfortunate enough to have been looking up at the time were blinded, many permanently.

On August 6 the city of Hiroshima virtually disappeared under a mushroom-shaped cloud.

The radiant heat of the blast burned their skin, the burns ranging from charring to various stages of blistering to something like a severe sunburn for those farther out. The shock wave coming immediately after the fireball tore the blistered skin from many burn victims. A college-age girl recalled seeing classmates whose "faces and everything were completely burned and they held their arms out in front of them like kangaroos with only their hands pointed downward; from their whole bodies something like thin paper is dangling—it is their peeled-off skin which hangs there."[56]

Those people not exposed directly to the blast suffered as well. Buildings by the hundreds burst into flame and collapsed. Block after block was leveled, with only a few buildings of reinforced concrete left standing. Those inside them who could escape into the streets did so with their clothes on fire and covered with jagged wounds from flying glass. Many headed to the river and died there. A fifth-grade boy remembered, "The river became not a stream of flowing water but rather a stream of drifting dead bodies. No matter how much I might exaggerate the stories of the burned people who died shrieking and of how the city of Hiroshima was burned to the ground, the facts would still be clearly more terrible."[57]

RADIATION POISONING

The suffering and dying lasted long after the fires had been extinguished. Survivors began to experience nausea, vomiting, and diarrhea. Their hair fell out, and they developed sores under the skin. Their bodies had absorbed massive amounts of gamma rays, destroying their ability to make fresh blood cells and cells needed to fight off infection. They weakened and died by the thousands. By the end of 1945, an estimated 140,000 people in Hiroshima had died, either during the bombing or from radiation sickness. Another 60,000 would die over the next five years from related causes such as leukemia and other forms of cancer.

FIGHT OR SURRENDER?

In Tokyo, arguments raged between the military and those who advocated surrender. As they argued, another Japanese city was destroyed. On August 9, just before midnight, the B-29 *Bocks Car*, piloted by Major Charles Sweeney, took off from

DEATH OF A CITY

The atom bomb blasts over Hiroshima and Nagasaki destroyed more than buildings and people. They ripped apart the cultural fabric of the two cities.

After the war, a Japanese committee compiled a lengthy study of the damage done by the atom bombs. Some of its findings, translated by Eisei Ishikawa and David Swain and published as *Hiroshima and Nagasaki,* are presented here.

> In the case of an atomic bombing . . . a community does not merely receive an impact; the community itself is destroyed. Within 2 kilometers [1.2 miles] of the atomic bomb's hypocenter all life and property were shattered, burned, and buried under ashes. The visible forms of the city where people once carried on their daily lives vanished without a trace. The destruction was sudden and thorough; there was virtually no chance to escape. . . . Citizens who had lost no family members in the holocaust [attack] were as rare as stars at sunrise. . . . The atomic bomb had blasted and burned hospitals, schools, city offices, police stations, and every other kind of human organization. . . . Family, relatives, neighbors, and friends relied on a broad range of interdependent organizations for everything from birth, marriage, and funerals to firefighting, productive work, and daily living. These traditional communities were completely demolished in an instant. . . . The whole of society was laid waste to its very foundations.

Tinian carrying a replica of the Fat Man that had been tested the previous month at Trinity. The intended target was Kokura, but the ground was obscured by haze and Sweeney decided to head for a secondary target, Nagasaki. That city was also obscured and it seemed that, with fuel running low, the mission might need to be called off. At almost the last moment, however, a hole opened up and the bombardier was able to zero in on a stadium.

Fat Man exploded above Nagasaki with the force of twenty-two tons of TNT. Since the target area was a valley bordered on either side by steep hills, the damage was less than at Hiroshima. Still, seventy thousand people were killed, and another seventy thousand died later.

This time, Japanese emperor Hirohito forced his generals to accept the inevitable. An offer to surrender was sent through the neutral Swiss and reached Washington on August 10. There would be more conventional bombing raids on Japan before a second offer was finally accepted on August 14, but there would be no more atom bombs. Vice President Henry Wallace said, Truman "didn't like the idea of killing, as he said, 'all those kids.'"[58]

MISSION ACCOMPLISHED

The atom bomb had done its job, cutting World War II short by a year or more. The Manhattan Project had fulfilled its promise, but at a tremendous cost—a cost measured in money and manpower on the American side and in death and destruction in Japan. As the Japanese in Hiroshima and Nagasaki buried their dead, Americans in Washington and Los Alamos celebrated.

On August 9 the B-29 Bocks Car *dropped a duplicate of Fat Man on Nagasaki. Soon afterwards Japan offered to surrender.*

The celebration at Los Alamos was noisier than most. George Kistiakowski, after several drinks, rigged up a twenty-one-gun salute using leftover cases of TNT.

Not everyone felt like celebrating, though. Before the Trinity test, Teller had written to Oppenheimer, saying, "I have no hope of clearing my conscience. The things we are working on are so terrible that no amount of protesting or fiddling with politics will save our souls."[59]

QUIETLY THANKFUL

Other Americans were celebrating with quiet thanksgiving. In training camps, onboard ships, and on islands scattered throughout the Pacific, thousands of soldiers, sailors, and marines knew there would be no invasion of Japan. Thousands of Japanese had died, but they, the Americans, would live. It had been with them in mind that Truman decided to use the atom bomb. "I could not worry about what history would say about my personal morality," he later wrote. "I made the only decision I ever knew how to make. I did what I thought was right."[60]

Truman publicly thanked the thousands of Americans who had been part of the Manhattan Project. "What has been done," he said, "is the greatest achievement of organized science in history. It was done under high pressure, and without failure. We have spent two billion dollars on the greatest scientific gamble in history—and won."[61]

Work at Los Alamos would continue. The city atop the New Mexico mesa would become a center for atomic research. For many who had labored there, however, the adventure was at an end. They went back to their university offices and laboratories.

Oppenheimer's last day was October 16, 1945. At a ceremony in which a special scroll of appreciation from the War Department was presented to him by General Groves, he stood on the steps of one of the old Los Alamos school buildings and told his colleagues,

> If atomic bombs are to be added to the arsenals of a warring world, or to the arsenals of nations preparing for war, then the time will come when mankind will curse the names of Los Alamos and Hiroshima. The peoples of this world must unite or they will perish. This war, that has ravaged so much of the earth, has written these

A PRISONER'S REMORSE

When word spread about the use of the atom bomb against Japan, many people who had been part of the Manhattan Project were troubled by the fact that their work had resulted in such a catastrophic loss of life. Their view was shared by scientists in other countries, some of whom had played important parts in the discoveries leading up to the manufacture of the bomb.

Otto Hahn, the German physicist who in 1938 had been the first to achieve fission without fully realizing what it was, had been captured and interned in Great Britain with other German scientists. In his autobiography *My Life*, Hahn describes his reaction to the news of the destruction of Hiroshima and Nagasaki.

> At first I refused to believe that this could be true, but in the end I had to face the fact that it was officially confirmed by the President of the United States. I was shocked and depressed beyond measure. The thought of the unspeakable misery of countless innocent women and children was something I could scarcely bear. After I had been given some gin to quiet my nerves, my fellow-prisoners were also told the news. . . . By the end of a long evening of discussion, attempts at explanation, and self-reproaches I was so agitated that Max von Laue [a fellow German scientist] and the others became seriously concerned on my behalf. They ceased worrying only at two o'clock in the morning, when they saw that I was asleep.

words. The atomic bomb has spelled them out for all men to understand. Other men have spoken them, in other times, of other wars, or other weapons. They have not prevailed. There are some, misled by a false sense of human history, who hold that they will not prevail today. It is not for us to believe that. By our works we are committed, committed to a world united, before this common peril, in law, and in humanity.[62]

Epilogue

Almost immediately after the atom bombs fell on Hiroshima and Nagasaki in the summer of 1945, the debate began, and it has continued ever since. Was the United States morally and/or militarily justified in dropping the bombs, given the destruction of two cities and the eventual loss of more than 300,000 Japanese lives?

Critics of the decision claim that the war would have come to a quick end without the use of nuclear weapons. They cite the saturation bombing that was reducing most major Japanese cities to rubble. They also cite evidence that many Japanese political leaders—and even some within the military—were reluctant to continue the war.

Those who support the decision quote the old Japanese saying "We will fight until we eat stones."[63] They describe the fanaticism of the Japanese, both soldiers and civilians, during the conquest of islands in the Pacific. They claim that only a successful, full-scale invasion of Japan would have forced a surrender, at the cost of as many as half a million American lives.

Such estimates, the counterargument goes, have been grossly exaggerated. The Japanese military had been so weakened that American casualties would have been limited to fewer than twenty-five thousand.

Any number of American deaths that could have been avoided, opponents counter, are too many. Certainly the fighting men and their families in 1945 would have held a less academic view on the death estimates than future historians. One soldier wrote,

> When the bombs dropped and news began to circulate that [the invasion of Japan] would not, after all, take place, that we would not be obliged to run up the beaches near Tokyo assault-firing while being mortared and shelled, for all the fake manliness of our facades we cried with relief and joy. We were going to live. We were going to grow into adulthood after all.[64]

GUESSWORK AND CERTAINTY

In fact, neither argument can be either proved or disproved. There is no sure way of knowing what might or might not have

Three men walk through the rubble of Tokyo after an air raid. Critics of the decision to use the atom bomb argued that saturation bombing using conventional weapons could have quickly ended the war.

led to a Japanese surrender. How many Americans, and Japanese, might have died during an invasion is pure guesswork. What is certain is that the atom bomb did bring World War II to a quick end. Little Boy fell on August 6, and Japan surrendered eight days later.

The true justification, if any, for the use of the atom bomb lies in the fact that, except for tests, it has never been used since. Indeed, even nuclear testing was banned toward the end of the twentieth century. Those who created the bomb were afraid of the power they had unleashed. Truman wrote, "We are only termites on a planet and maybe when we bore too deeply into the planet there'll be a reckoning—who knows?"[65]

In fact, the atom bomb and its successor, the thermonuclear or hydrogen bomb, were essentially too powerful to be employed as a weapon of war. Some of the more thoughtful people involved with the Manhattan Project knew this. Niels Bohr, although opposed to using the bomb, wrote about the changes it would bring about. Major wars, he forecast, would cease to be fought because there could be no winners, only the destruction of all sides.

AWAKENING THE WORLD

Harvard University president James Conant, a member of President Roosevelt's original Top Policy Group in 1941, saw the atom bomb as "the only way to awaken the world to the necessity of abolishing war altogether."[66] And even a warhorse like General Groves could see that, in bringing about the end to one war, he had prevented other, perhaps more deadly conflicts. "Was the development of the atomic bomb by the United States necessary?" he wrote. "Unequivocally, yes. The atomic bomb is what has kept the peace since 1945."[67]

Today a monument stands at ground zero of the Trinity test site. After the war, General Groves wrote that the atom bomb had kept the peace since 1945.

Thus, for many, the long-term justification for the United States's use of the atom bomb in World War II is that the sacrifice of hundreds of thousands of Japanese might well have prevented the slaughter of millions of people around the world in future years, future wars. It brought humankind face to face with the knowledge that the technology of war had gone too far and threatened to escape the control of those who wielded it. In a commencement speech in 1946, Oppenheimer said,

> It did not take atomic weapons to make war terrible. . . .
> It did not take atomic weapons to make man want peace, a peace that would last. But the atomic bomb was the turn of the screw. It has made the prospect of future war unendurable. It has led us up those last few steps to the mountain pass; and beyond there is a different country.[68]

NOTES

Introduction

1. Quoted in William L. Laurence, *Dawn over Zero.* New York: Alfred A. Knopf, 1947, p. 193.

2. Quoted in Lansing Lamont, *Day of Trinity.* New York: Atheneum, 1965, p. 226.

3. Quoted in Peter Goodchild, *J. Robert Oppenheimer: Shatterer of Worlds.* Boston: Houghton Mifflin, 1981, p. 161.

4. I. I. Rabi, *Science: The Center of Culture.* New York: World Publishing, 1970, p. 138.

5. Quoted in James W. Kunetka, *City of Fire.* Englewood Cliffs, NJ: Prentice-Hall, 1978, p. 170.

Chapter 1: Dividing the Indivisible

6. Quoted in Robert W. Conn, "Atoms: Their Structure, Properties, and Component Particles," in *The New Encyclopaedia Britannica.* Chicago: Encyclopaedia Britannica, 1998, p. 672.

7. Quoted in Richard Rhodes, *The Making of the Atomic Bomb.* New York: Simon and Schuster, 1986, p. 31.

8. Quoted in Rhodes, *The Making of the Atomic Bomb,* p. 43.

9. Quoted in Arthur S. Eve, *Rutherford.* New York: Macmillan, 1939, p. 102.

10. Quoted in Rhodes, *The Making of the Atomic Bomb,* p. 44.

11. Quoted in G. K. T. Conn and H. D. Turner, *The Evolution of the Nuclear Atom.* London: Iliffe Books, 1966, p. 136.

12. Quoted in Rhodes, *The Making of the Atomic Bomb,* p. 137.

13. Quoted in Rhodes, *The Making of the Atomic Bomb,* p. 164.

14. Quoted in Rhodes, *The Making of the Atomic Bomb,* p. 165.

Chapter 2: Acceleration

15. Quoted in Rhodes, *The Making of the Atomic Bomb,* p. 214.

16. Quoted in Rhodes, *The Making of the Atomic Bomb,* p. 253.

17. Quoted in Rhodes, *The Making of the Atomic Bomb,* p. 263.

18. Leo Szilard, *Leo Szilard: His Version of the Facts.* Ed. Spencer R. Weart and Gertrude Weiss Szilard. Cambridge, MA: MIT Press, 1978, p. 53.

19. Quoted in Rhodes, *The Making of the Atomic Bomb,* p. 314.

20. Edward Teller, *Energy from Heaven and Earth*. San Francisco: W. H. Freeman, 1979, p. 145.

21. Quoted in Rhodes, *The Making of the Atomic Bomb*, p. 323.

22. Quoted in Jane Wilson, ed., *All in Our Time: The Reminiscences of Twelve Nuclear Pioneers*. Chicago: Bulletin of the Atomic Scientists, 1975, p. 55.

23. Arthur Holly Compton, *Atomic Quest*. New York: Oxford University Press, 1956, p. 49.

24. Quoted in Rhodes, *The Making of the Atomic Bomb*, p. 386.

25. Quoted in Rhodes, *The Making of the Atomic Bomb*, p. 406.

26. Quoted in Rhodes, *The Making of the Atomic Bomb*, p. 439.

27. Quoted in Wilson, *All in Our Time*, p. 95.

28. Eugene P. Wigner, *Symmetries and Reflections*. Cambridge, MA: MIT Press, 1970, p. 240.

Chapter 3: The Gadget

29. Quoted in Rhodes, *The Making of the Atomic Bomb*, p. 424.

30. Quoted in Lamont, *Day of Trinity*, p. 46.

31. Quoted in Kunetka, *City of Fire*, p. 40.

32. Quoted in Rhodes, *The Making of the Atomic Bomb*, p. 448.

33. Quoted in Ferenc Morton Szasz, *The Day the Sun Rose Twice*. Albuquerque: University of New Mexico Press, 1984, p. 21.

34. Quoted in Nuel Pharr Davis, *Lawrence and Oppenheimer*. New York: Simon and Schuster, 1968, p. 173.

35. Quoted in Davis, *Lawrence and Oppenheimer*, p. 216.

36. Rhodes, *The Making of the Atomic Bomb*, p. 480.

Chapter 4: Trinity

37. Quoted in Goodchild, *J. Robert Oppenheimer*, p. 118.

38. Otto Frisch, *What Little I Remember*. New York: Cambridge University Press, 1979, p. 161.

39. Quoted in Rhodes, *The Making of the Atomic Bomb*, p. 575.

40. Quoted in Goodchild, *J. Robert Oppenheimer*, p. 151.

41. Quoted in Rhodes, *The Making of the Atomic Bomb*, p. 657.

42. Quoted in Wilson, *All in Our Time*, p. 185.

43. Quoted in Goodchild, *J. Robert Oppenheimer*, p. 155.

44. Quoted in Szasz, *The Day the Sun Rose Twice*, p. 76.

Chapter 5: Pika-Don

45. Quoted in Rhodes, *The Making of the Atomic Bomb*, p. 584.

46. Quoted in Rhodes, *The Making of the Atomic Bomb*, p. 681.

47. Quoted in J. Samuel Walker, *Prompt and Utter Destruction*. Chapel Hill: University of North Carolina Press, 1997, p. 13.

48. Quoted in Walker, *Prompt and Utter Destruction*, p. 43.

49. Quoted in Len Giovannitti and Fred Freed, *The Decision to Drop the Bomb*. London: Methuen, 1967, p. 104.

50. Quoted in Walker, *Prompt and Utter Destruction*, p. 65.

51. Leslie R. Groves, *Now It Can Be Told*. New York: Harper & Row, 1962, p. 267.

52. Quoted in Walker, *Prompt and Utter Destruction*, p. 72.

53. Quoted in Rhodes, *The Making of the Atomic Bomb*, p. 693.

54. Quoted in Joseph L. Marx, *Seven Hours to Zero*. New York: Putnam, 1967, p. 106.

55. Quoted in Rhodes, *The Making of the Atomic Bomb*, p. 711.

56. Quoted in Arata Osada, ed., *Children of the A-Bomb*. Trans. Jean Dan and Ruth Sieben-Morgen. Ann Arbor, MI: Midwest Publishers International, 1982, p. 313.

57. Quoted in Osada, *Children of the A-Bomb*, p. 219.

58. Quoted in Walker, *Prompt and Utter Destruction*, p. 86.

59. Quoted in Rhodes, *The Making of the Atomic Bomb*, p. 697.

60. Quoted in Lamont, *Day of Trinity*, p. 303.

61. Quoted in Goodchild, *J. Robert Oppenheimer*, p. 169.

62. Quoted in Kunetka, *City of Fire*, p. 203.

Epilogue

63. Quoted in Rhodes, *The Making of the Atomic Bomb*, p. 597.

64. Quoted in Rhodes, *The Making of the Atomic Bomb*, p. 736.

65. Quoted in Rhodes, *The Making of the Atomic Bomb*, p. 683.

66. Quoted in Walker, *Prompt and Utter Destruction*, p. 101.

67. Quoted in Lamont, *Day of Trinity*, p. 309.

68. Quoted in Rhodes, *The Making of the Atomic Bomb*, p. 778.

FOR FURTHER READING

Books

Peter Goodchild, *J. Robert Oppenheimer: Shatterer of Worlds.* Boston: Houghton Mifflin, 1981. Absorbing, highly readable biography of the man who directed the research on and manufacture of the first atom bombs.

Stéphane Groueff, *Manhattan Project.* Boston: Little, Brown, 1967. Detailed account of the events that led to the building of the atom bomb, the decision to use it, and the aftermath.

Leslie R. Groves, *Now It Can Be Told.* New York: Harper & Row, 1962. Entertaining autobiographical account of the development of the atom bomb by the general who directed the project.

Lansing Lamont, *Day of Trinity.* New York: Atheneum, 1965. Comprehensive account of the test of the first atom bomb and the events leading up to it.

William L. Laurence, *Dawn over Zero.* New York: Alfred A. Knopf, 1947. The story of the development of the atom bomb by the only journalist allowed to witness its first test.

Victoria Sherrow, *The Making of the Atom Bomb.* San Diego, CA: Lucent Books, 2000. A detailed history of the events leading up to and the detonation of the atom bomb.

Ferenc Morton Szasz, *The Day the Sun Rose Twice.* Albuquerque: University of New Mexico Press, 1984. Lively account of the development of the atom bomb with special attention to the Trinity test.

Web Sites

A-Bomb WWW Museum www.csi.ad.jp/ABOMB/. Japanese web site devoted to the bombing of Hiroshima and Nagasaki. Includes articles, photographs, and recordings of voices of survivors.

Los Alamos National Laboratory http://ext.lanl.gov/worldview/ welcome/history.html. Includes articles written for the 50th anniversary of Los Alamos National Laboratory, documents on the decision to use the atom bombs, history and photographs of the Trinity test site, and personal recollections of survivors of Hiroshima.

WORKS CONSULTED

Pierre Biquard, *Frederic Joliot-Curie*. New York: Eriksson, 1962. Biography of the son-in-law of Pierre and Marie Curie, who, with his wife Irene, made many important discoveries in chemistry.

Stanley A. Blumberg and Gwinn Owens, *Energy and Conflict: The Life and Times of Edward Teller*. New York: G. P. Putnam's Sons, 1976. Comprehensive biography of the Hungarian-born physicist who helped develop the atomic bomb and, later, the hydrogen bomb.

Stanley A. Blumberg and Louis G. Panos, *Edward Teller: Giant of the Golden Age of Physics*. New York: Charles Scribner's Sons, 1990. Biography of Teller with particular emphasis on his role in Cold War politics and the development of the hydrogen bomb.

John W. Campbell, *The Atomic Story*. New York: Henry Holt, 1947. The history of nuclear physics and the development of atomic weapons in simple, easy-to-understand language.

Committee for the Compilation of Materials on Damage Caused by the Atomic Bombs in Hiroshima and Nagasaki, *Hiroshima and Nagasaki*. Trans. by Eisei Ishikawa and David L. Swain. New York: BasicBooks, 1981. Findings of a Japanese committee that studied the effects of the atom bombs dropped on the two Japanese cities.

Arthur Holly Compton, *Atomic Quest*. New York: Oxford University Press, 1956. Firsthand account of the development of the atom bomb by the University of Chicago president who was among the key figures.

G. K. T. Conn and H. D. Turner, *The Evolution of the Nuclear Atom*. London: Iliffe Books, 1966. Traces the development of nuclear physics and the discoveries of various atomic components.

Robert W. Conn, "Atoms: Their Structure, Properties, and Component Particles." In *The New Encyclopaedia Britannica*. Chicago: Encyclopaedia Britannica, 1998. Comprehensive overview of scientific research into atomic structure.

Nuel Pharr Davis, *Lawrence and Oppenheimer*. New York: Simon and Schuster, 1968. Entertaining examination of the roles of and interactions between two of the leading scientists in the development of the atom bomb.

Arthur S. Eve, *Rutherford.* New York: Macmillan, 1939. Biography of the British physicist whose discoveries were key to the development of the atom bomb.

Otto Frisch, *What Little I Remember.* New York: Cambridge University Press, 1979. Autobiography of one of the central figures in the discovery of nuclear fission.

George Gamow, *Thirty Years That Shook Physics.* Garden City, NY: Doubleday, 1966. The story of the development of the quantum theory of matter and its effect on the understanding of the universe.

Len Giovannitti and Fred Freed, *The Decision to Drop the Bomb.* London: Methuen, 1967. Insightful examination of the factors that led to the American decision to employ the atom bomb against Japan.

Michihiko Hachiya, *Hiroshima Diary.* Trans. Warner Wells. Chapel Hill: University of North Carolina Press, 1955. Graphic and disturbing eyewitness account of the devastation of Hiroshima by the atom bomb.

Otto Hahn, *My Life.* Trans. Ernst Kaiser and Eithne Wilkins. London: Macdonald, 1970. Autobiography of the German atomic scientist.

Julia E. Johnsen, ed., *The Atomic Bomb.* New York: H. W. Wilson, 1946. Compilation of newspaper and magazine articles dealing with atomic energy and nuclear weapons.

James W. Kunetka, *City of Fire.* Englewood Cliffs, NJ: Prentice-Hall, 1978. Highly readable account of life and work at Los Alamos from 1943 to 1945.

Joseph L. Marx, *Seven Hours to Zero.* New York: Putnam, 1967. Comprehensive account of the mission against Hiroshima.

Arata Osada, ed., *Children of the A-Bomb.* Trans. Jean Dan and Ruth Sieben-Morgen. Ann Arbor, MI: Midwest Publishers International, 1982. Personal recollections of children who survived the bombing of Hiroshima and Nagasaki.

I. I. Rabi, *Science: The Center of Culture.* New York: World Publishing, 1970. Treatise on the central importance of science as a sociological force written by one of the physicists prominent in the development of the atom bomb.

Richard Rhodes, *The Making of the Atomic Bomb*. New York: Simon and Schuster, 1986. Massive account of the development and use of the atom bomb; an excellent mix of science and the personalities behind it.

Emilio Segrè, *Enrico Fermi: Physicist*. Chicago: University of Chicago Press, 1970. Biography, written by a countryman and colleague, of one of the greatest and most colorful physicists of the twentieth century.

Albert Speer, *Inside the Third Reich*. Trans. Richard and Clara Winston. New York: Bonanza Books, 1982. Memoirs of the man who was one of Adolf Hitler's closest associates toward the end of World War II.

Leo Szilard, *Leo Szilard: His Version of the Facts*. Ed. Spencer R. Weart and Gertrude Weiss Szilard. Cambridge, MA: MIT Press, 1978. Personal recollections and correspondence of the physicist who was one of the most vocal about the dangers of the atom bomb.

Edward Teller, *Energy from Heaven and Earth*. San Francisco: W. H. Freeman, 1979. The noted nuclear physicist presents his view of energy and how humanity puts it to use for both good and evil.

Gordon Thomas and Max Morgan Witts, *Enola Gay*. New York: Stein and Day, 1977. Entertaining account of the mission to drop the atom bomb on Hiroshima.

J. Samuel Walker, *Prompt and Utter Destruction*. Chapel Hill: University of North Carolina Press, 1997. Interesting account of the various factors considered by President Harry Truman in his decision to use the atom bomb on Japan.

Eugene P. Wigner, *Symmetries and Reflections*. Cambridge, MA: MIT Press, 1970. Series of scientific essays by one of the physicists involved in the Manhattan Project.

Jane Wilson, ed., *All in Our Time: The Reminiscences of Twelve Nuclear Pioneers*. Chicago: Bulletin of the Atomic Scientists, 1975. Personal views of most of the leading figures in the development of nuclear energy.

INDEX

magnetism, 17, 37–38

Making of the Atomic Bomb, The (Rhodes), 17

Manhattan Engineer District Office, 41

Manhattan Project
conclusion of, 92–93
naming of, 41
revealed to Truman, 79
see also atom bomb; gun bomb; implosion bomb

Marsden, Ernest, 22, 24

Marshall, George, 84

Martin Aircraft, 78

MAUD, 39–40

Maxwell, James Clerk, 17

McDaniel, Bryce, 73

McMillan, Edwin, 38

Meitner, Lise, 28, 31–33, 63

Military Policy Committee, 46, 54

Morrison, Philip, 26

My Life (Hahn), 94

Nagaoka, Hantaro, 21

Nagasaki, Japan, 91–92

National Academy of Science, 39

National Defense Research Council, 39–40

Nazi Germany
competition to develop atom bomb, 27, 28, 34, 45
end of war in Europe, 70, 81
see also World War II

Neddermeyer, Seth
detonation design by, 57–58
research by
on explosives, 61
on implosion bomb, 65–68

neptunium, 38

Neumann, John von, 55, 61, 65–68

neutrons
discovery of, 25–27
see also nuclear fission

Newton, Isaac, 14, 17

nitrogen, 25

nuclear fission, 31–34
plutonium discovery, 38
research by Oppenheimer, 53

nuclei
discovery of, 22–24

Oak Ridge, Tennessee
choice for U-235 production site, 49–50
conditions at, 51–52

Office of Scientific Research and Development (OSRD), 39, 40

Oppenheimer, J. Robert, 11–13
on atom bomb, 98
bomb assembly research supervised by, 52–54
on bombing of Japan, 82
characteristics of, 57
farewell speech at Los Alamos, 93–94
on living conditions at Los Alamos, 64–65
Trinity test, 72, 74

Oppenheimer, Kitty, 54

paraffin, 25–26, 32

Parsons, Deke, 58, 61–63, 87

peace
as result of bomb, 97–98

Pearl Harbor, 40

Pegram, George, 34

Peierls, Rudolf, 36–37

phosphorus, 28

Physics (Aristotle), 15

pika-don ("flash-boom"), 89

pitchblende, 18

Planck, Max, 23

"plug," 73

"plum pudding" model, 21

plutonium, 38
complications of using, 58–60, 62
production of, 46–49
research on, 41–42

PICTURE CREDITS

ABOUT THE AUTHOR

William W. Lace is a native of Fort Worth, Texas. He holds a bachelor's degree from Texas Christian University, a master's from East Texas State University, and a doctorate from the University of North Texas. After working for newspapers in Baytown, Texas and Fort Worth, he joined the University of Texas at Arlington as sports information director and later became the director of the news service. He is now executive assistant to the chancellor for the Tarrant County College District in Fort Worth. He and his wife, Laura, live in Arlington and have two children. Lace has written numerous other works for Lucent Books, one of which—*The Death Camps* in the Holocaust Library series—was selected by the New York Public Library for its 1999 Recommended Teenage Reading List.